MOVED BY FAITH

MOVED BY FAITH

STORIES FROM American Catholic Radio

JUDY ZARICK

ST. ANTHONY MESSENGER PRESS
Cincinnati, Ohio

Scripture passages have been taken from *New Revised Standard Version Bible,* copyright ©1989 by the Division of Christian Education of the National Council of the Churches of Christ in the U.S.A., and used by permission. All rights reserved.

Cover and book design by Mark Sullivan
Cover image © Veer | Ocean Photography

LIBRARY OF CONGRESS CATALOGING-IN-PUBLICATION DATA
Moved by faith : stories from American Catholic radio / Judy Zarick.
    p. cm.
   ISBN 978-1-61636-323-9 (alk. paper)
 1. American Catholic radio. 2. Radio in religion—United States. 3. Radio in religion—Catholic Church. I. Zarick, Judy. II. American Catholic radio.
              BV655.2.U6M68 2012
                  282'.73—dc23
                                2011051611

ISBN 978-1-61636-323-9

Copyright ©2012, by St. Anthony Messenger Press. All rights reserved.

Published by St. Anthony Messenger Press
28 W. Liberty St.
Cincinnati, OH 45202
www.AmericanCatholic.org
www.SAMPBooks.org

Printed in the United States of America.
Printed on acid-free paper.

12 13 14 15 16   5 4 3 2 1

CONTENTS

INTRODUCTION
  A Note From the Producer | *ix*

CHAPTER ONE
Abraham and Isaac: From Despair to Hope
  Baby Not Breathing *Tim Jaccard* | *1*
  A Walk of Faith *Kelly Ann Lynch* | *5*
  Pornography—It Hurts Us All *Sam and Beth Meier* | *8*
  Don't Wait, Just Do It *Patricia Oetting* | *12*
  Parched and Redeemed *Heather King* | *15*
  Moved to Action: Questions for Thought | *18*

CHAPTER TWO
The Plight of Job: Remaining Faithful Against All Odds
  Survivor's Guilt *Michael Nolte* | *19*
  Jesus, Save Us! *Robert Rogers* | *23*
  A Silent Killer *Patricia Gallagher* | *26*
  Choose to Pick Up Your Cross *John Foppe* | *30*
  Moved to Action: Questions for Thought | *32*

CHAPTER THREE
The Conversion of Saul: Finding a Home in the Church
  Smart People Don't Believe in God *Jennifer Fulwiler* | *33*
  Prison Time Is Thinking Time *Joseph Pearce* | *37*
  Multiple Miracles *Kari Beckman* | *40*
  Death of the Innocents *Steven Mosher* | *43*
  My Guru Mentor *Tucker Coon* | *46*
  Moved to Action: Questions for Thought | *49*

CHAPTER FOUR
From Shepherd Boy to King David: Drastic Job Changes
　I'm All Shook Up *Sr. Mary Ann Foggin, s.g.l.* | 51
　Living Life Six Feet Under *Dale Robinson* | 55
　The American Dream…in Haiti? *Deacon Patrick Moynihan* | 58
　You Can Call Me Mister, Doctor, Father *Fr. Don Forsythe* | 61
　The Thrill of Victory *Chase Hilgenbrinck* | 63
　Moved to Action: Questions for Thought | 66

CHAPTER FIVE
The Wisdom of Solomon: Thinking Outside the Box
　The Almighty Dollar *Jill Kohler* | 67
　Mary's Special Touch *Cheri Lomonte* | 70
　Extreme Makeover Catholic-Style *Fr. Jonathan Licari* | 73
　What's a Nice Jew Doing at the Vatican? *Sir Gilbert Levine* | 76
　Send in the Clowns *Gilbert and Charlotte Ardoin* | 79
　Moved to Action: Questions for Thought | 82

CHAPTER SIX
The Good Samaritan: Who Is My Neighbor?
　Planting Roots of Peace *Heidi and Kyleigh Kühn* | 83
　Do It for the Children *Debbie Cornall* | 86
　My Faith Will Build It *Lucious Newsom* | 89
　Dying of Thirst *Brenda Koinis* | 92
　Moved to Action: Questions for Thought | 95

CHAPTER SEVEN
Womb to Tomb: Pro-life for All Life
   Gabriel's Gift *JoAnne Cascia* | *97*
   Choose Life, No Matter What *Edel Carrick* | *101*
   Always Listen to Your Mother *Dr. John Bruchalski* | *104*
   This Can't Be Happening *Lisa Gigliotti* | *107*
   "You Do It." "Who, Me?" *Karen Bussey* | *110*
   Moved to Action: Questions for Thought | *113*

CHAPTER EIGHT
For the Least of These: Living Justly Today
   Building a Simple House *Clark Massey* | *115*
   Home Away From Home *Tina Marquart* | *119*
   Takin' It to the Streets *Deacon John Green* | *122*
   Who's Watching the Kids? *Holly Schlaack* | *125*
   A Little Tender Loving Care *Alice Wold* | *128*
   Moved to Action: Questions for Thought | *131*

CONCLUSION
One More Thought Before You Go | *133*

INTRODUCTION

A NOTE FROM THE PRODUCER

American Catholic Radio (ACR), which is funded by the United States Conference of Catholic Bishops (USCCB) and corporate sponsors, is a weekly half-hour show that informs and inspires in the popular style of the Franciscans. Each week *ACR* draws its inspiration from the liturgical season, current events, and popular Catholic topics.

ACR can be heard on many Catholic radio stations across the country, on *The Catholic Channel* on SiriusXM Satellite Radio and at our website: http://productions.franciscanmedia.org.

ACR's goal is to be both timely and timeless. You'll find the wisdom of the saints, the rich tradition of the Church's liturgy and practice, the thoughts of contemporary Church leaders and thinkers, the faith and actions of contemporary Catholics—both lay and ordained—as well as quiet moments for reflection. Each program is built around two extended interviews. Other segments offer continuing features. And all shows are presented in harmony with Church teaching.

On *American Catholic Radio*, I produce a segment called "Living Faith." It spotlights individual Catholics who put their faith into action in interesting and dynamic ways, through their local parish, service organizations, families, and workplaces. Each week these interviews bring challenging examples of Catholics expressing their faith, inviting listeners to do likewise in their own lives. In essence, these people are taking the message of Jesus Christ and "putting shoes on the gospel."

I've had the privilege of working on *American Catholic Radio* since 2004. I never imagined the number of amazing people I would encounter in my search for a "great" interview for our "Living Faith" segment. At first I thought that finding fifty-two people a year might pose some difficulty. My goal was to find ordinary Catholics living out their faith. I wasn't looking for high-powered intellectuals and religious persons whose presence is splashed across newspapers and magazines. I wasn't looking for the next saint. I wanted to find people in the pew to whom I could relate—everyday Catholics who were doing something to put their faith into action. Boy, did I find them. I found people from all across the country, young and old, black and white, married and single, vowed religious, you name it. And as I interviewed person after person I became more and more convicted in my faith. I felt challenged to get up and start doing something to put my faith into action. The problem was that I was feeling like that *every* week. I couldn't stop talking about my interviews and sharing their wonderful stories with everyone who would listen. (My husband and kids listened to quite a few through many a family dinner.)

Now I'd like for you to feel what I experienced—to be challenged, to be motivated. And to be inspired to live out your faith in the unique way to which God calls you. My hope is that maybe one of these stories will inspire you to take that leap and say yes to however God is calling you in your life.

Judy Zarick
January 27, 2012

CHAPTER | ONE

ABRAHAM AND ISAAC
From Despair to Hope

Then Abraham reached out his hand and took the knife to kill his son. But the angel of the LORD called to him from heaven, and said, "Abraham, Abraham!" And he said, "Here I am." He said, "Do not lay your hand on the boy or do anything to him; for now I know that you fear God, since you have not withheld your son, your only son, from me."

—Genesis 22:10–12

BABY NOT BREATHING

Fifty-seven-year-old Tim Jaccard is a police medic, similar to a paramedic, for the Nassau County Police Department on Long Island, New York. But being a medic and dealing with emergencies on a daily basis didn't prepare him for the series of events he experienced in 1998.

Tim was on the job when he received a call on a "baby not breathing." He responded to the Hempstead court house.

"When I arrived," says Tim, "I found a 6-pound 4-ounce baby girl drowned in the toilet bowl by her mother. Three weeks later I responded to another 'baby not breathing' call and found a child wrapped in a plastic bag buried near an office complex in Albertson. Two weeks after that there was another 'baby not breathing' call—a child wrapped in a plastic bag buried in a backyard by his mother. And three weeks after that, responding to yet another 'baby not breathing' call, I found another child, wrapped in a plastic bag in a recycling bin."

Tim says he felt at that point that he was being sent a message, and he knew something had to be done. These were not the first abandoned babies he had been called to find, but never before had he experienced so many in such a short span of time. In addition to that, his daughter, Mary, had just had a miscarriage an hour before that first call had come in 1998. Tim knew he was being called to action.

"I believe that in my heart and soul I was angry with God at the time," he says. "There was my daughter, looking to get pregnant, and she had to go through a miscarriage. At the same time, I'm holding in my arms this child that the mother drowned. It wasn't fair. From there, I think He sent a message to me.

"Through research, I found that I could become what is known as a 'health proxy' to this child. That would give me the right to be able to treat the child medically. In this case, the only thing I could do for this baby was to give it dignity, and a name, and a proper burial."

Tim named the first baby he found Angelica. He also named the other children he found, took custody, and bought burial plots for them at the cemetery. He established a nonprofit foundation, AMT Children of Hope, to help pay for the funerals. *AMT* stands for *ambulance medical technician*.

"Now we handle the burials of any abandoned babies even if the mother is known and the baby is abandoned in the hospital," Tim says. "In the same ten-month period after I found baby Angelica, we had had forty-one newborn infants abandoned in only three cities: Houston, Mobile, and New York. Forty-one babies in a ten-month period had been victims of infanticide. That's when I started. I sat down and I wrote a bill."

Tim's bill was put forth for legislation. It was called the Infant Abandonment Protection Act, known by some as the Safe Haven Law. It allows a mother to relinquish her child at a safe place without worrying about criminal charges of abandonment.

"When I first started, all I wanted to do was give these babies dignity," Tim explains. "But after doing that, God sent me a second message. 'Hey,' He said, 'I want this stopped.' So then I started the crisis center and started moving in that direction. My mission here is now to try to reduce the number of deaths that occur."

Tim established the National Safe Haven Alliance and Hot Line in Washington, D.C. New York used to average sixteen to seventeen infant deaths from abandonment a year. Because of Tim's bill and crisis centers, they now average only three. There have been more than two thousand calls on their crisis line.

Tim explains the program: "A birth mother has an option to make a parenting plan, an adoption plan, and a relinquishment plan. We want to make sure we give that young woman every opportunity to make those other decisions. The last resort is the relinquishment. One thousand one hundred and twenty babies have been safely relinquished in the programs. Locally, we are up to ninety-six babies."

As difficult as it was to get his bill passed in New York, it was only the beginning of an even longer journey for Tim.

"I had no idea I was going to have to go from state to state," he says. "Every state has a different policy. And it's not a federal bill unless it's unified within the states where every state has a safe-haven bill. We then can go back and ask Congress to unify all the state bills with the blessings of each individual state. And that's presently what we really want to do."

Only Alaska and Nebraska have yet to agree to some form of Tim's proposed bill. Along with his wife, Aedan, who serves as nurse coordinator for the program, Tim and many qualified volunteers from all over the country have helped thousands of troubled women and their children.

"My faith has been stronger in my belief that what I'm doing is the right thing," Tim says. "And I think He's directing me to do the things that I do."

Tim is truly living out his faith and bringing hope and dignity to some of the most vulnerable.

Tim Jaccard is the founder and president of the AMT Children of Hope Foundation. He is the advocate and author of a bill, the Infant Abandonment Protection Act, first passed in Texas and, since this story first aired, has been adopted by all fifty states across the nation. He's married and has three children and five grandchildren. He continues to work endlessly and passionately to educate and prevent the abandonment of infants. Find his nonprofit at www.amtchildrenofhope.com. | Aired: October 8, 2007

A Walk of Faith

Of the many riveting images to come out of the tragedy of 9/11, one of the most memorable was the sight of Fr. Mychal Judge, O.F.M., being carried out of the rubble by New York City firefighters. He died when the first tower collapsed and was the first recorded victim of this horrific tragedy.

Kelly Ann Lynch and her family were good friends of Fr. Mychal, who was chaplain to the firefighters of New York City.

"We were just devastated," Kelly says. "We felt lost. We felt like sheep without a shepherd, really. We didn't know what we were going to do and how we were going to go on without him guiding us and just being there. I mean he was there for us all throughout our life."

Fr. Mychal was especially present when Kelly's first child, her daughter Shannon, became severely ill with a rare liver disease at six weeks of age. The doctors were not hopeful about the outcome; they told Kelly that Shannon would probably die by her second birthday.

"It was a very difficult time," Kelly recalls. "And the first person I called, of course, was Fr. Mychal. He was the one who guided us. He took us to the next phase where we needed to be. I was twenty-three at the time. I was a new young mother, and Fr. Mychal said, 'Well, you just have to give that baby back to God.' And I said, 'What do you mean give that baby back to God? He gave her to me.' He said, 'It's very simple. Once you figure out how to do it you will see how simple it is.' Once I let go, the doors began to open, and that's when we found out about an experimental procedure being done in Chicago."

Doctors were able to transplant part of Kelly's healthy liver into her daughter, and the procedure worked. Today, Shannon, eighteen, is living life and getting ready to go off to college.

After the events of 9/11, Kelly and her family struggled, as did so many others, with the pain and anger that gripped their lives after the loss of their friend.

"We needed to figure out how to forgive and move forward," she says. "And we didn't have Fr. Mychal to show us how to do it. In the end it really was Shannon, who was eleven at the time, who showed us the way, through the gifts of the Holy Spirit and probably a little prompting from Fr. Mychal from above."

On the anniversary of her life-saving liver transplant, Shannon celebrated in typical fashion, with a party complete with cake and presents. But the January after Fr. Mychal died, she decided to do things differently. She approached her mother.

"Mom," she said. "I have an idea. How about if we collect socks for the homeless instead of presents for me this year? I'll ask all my friends to bring socks for the homeless and this way we can celebrate my life while we remember Fr. Mychal's."

With the help of friends and family, they collected fifteen hundred pairs of socks and sent them to St. Francis of Assisi parish in New York City, for distribution to the homeless.

The next message Kelly felt God had for her was to write a book about Fr. Mychal's life.

"I was hearing words in my soul and my heart and my being that were saying, 'He said *yes*, he said *yes*,'" Kelly says. "And as I heard the words, I was picturing Fr. Mychal's story. How he was a little boy in Brooklyn and how he said *yes* to shining shoes to help his family. And how he said *yes* to the AIDS patients and *yes* to the recovering alcoholics and, ultimately, on September 11, how he said *yes* to his firefighters and to those who needed him most."

Kelly wrote the book. And beyond that, she, her daughter Shannon, and their whole family have continued to honor Fr. Mychal's memory. They've expanded their sock ministry to the poor to include underwear.

They call it Blessed Bloomers, and the package includes an undershirt, two pairs of underwear, and a pair of socks.

"Everything that we give to our homeless brothers and sisters is new, and it's all about helping them to restore and maintain their own dignity," Kelly explains.

For the seventh year in a row, they'll be handing out Blessed Bloomers on September 11 to the homeless men and women in New York City who need their help. Kelly's award-winning children's book, *He Said Yes: The Story of Father Mychal Judge*, is also raising funds to help the homeless. Kelly has taken a horrible tragedy and turned it into something positive that all began with Fr. Mychal's example of saying *yes* to God.

"It's much easier not to dwell on *How am I going to forgive?* Or *How did these people do such a horrible thing?* That's part of it. Part of it, too, is not asking 'Why?' but just doing—getting out there and doing God's work and asking what He wants of you every day. The other part of it is to realize that people in general are more alike than they are not alike."

Kelly has a favorite prayer that she learned from Fr. Mychal. She feels it sums up how he led his life and how we should all be living as people of faith.

> *Lord, take me where you want me to go.*
> *Let me meet who you want me to meet.*
> *Tell me what you want me to say.*
> *And keep me out of your way.*

"If Fr. Mychal had lived through 9/11, he would have shown us how to forgive," Kelly believes. "He just walked a walk of faith, accepting whatever God's will was and allowing God to use him every day."

Kelly Ann Lynch is a stay-at-home mother, a bestselling and award-winning author, a cofounder of Mychal's Message, and the founder of Sandal Steps Presentations. Born and raised Catholic, Kelly is also a Secular Franciscan. | *Aired: September 8, 2008*

***

Pornography—It Hurts Us All

According to research from the journal *Sexual Addiction and Compulsivity*, pornography revenue in the United States exceeds the combined revenues of all professional football, baseball, and basketball franchises combined. And the United States is the world's top producer of both Internet pornography and pornographic videos. To say the least, it's a problem. And Sam Meier, from Kansas City, Kansas, was not immune to its effects. Before he met his future wife, Beth, he was struggling.

"I'd had many problems with pornography before Beth and I met, starting back in middle school," he says. "And those problems continued throughout junior high and high school. In college, things started improving with my faith life. And Beth and I went to Rome for a semester and really started praying more and getting connected to the Church. I assumed that those problems with pornography would just go away when we got married. But within two months of getting married, coming home, and getting the Internet set up, it became a pretty big problem."

Sam's addiction to pornography wasn't just affecting his own life, it was having a major impact on his marriage. "It consumed him," says Beth. "He was looking at this stuff at work; I was worried that he might lose his job. And I caught him several times late at night. I could tell by his body language. He was for the most part open and wanted to share it with me. So I was very fortunate, if you can call it that. At least he wasn't trying to hide it from me. But it was a huge strain on the first two years of our marriage."

Sam's problem with pornography was creeping into every aspect of his life. He recalls: "During that time when I became more involved with Internet pornography, I not only withdrew from Beth but I also became very isolated and stopped spending time with my family and friends. I was just filled with a lot of shame. I became more reclusive and didn't answer calls. It was like I was on my own island in the apartment."

Beth and Sam decided to look for help. They didn't feel their friends and family had the answers. Some of them didn't even think there was much to be concerned with in the first place. So together they looked for a counselor. "It took a while to find the right people to help out," says Sam. "One of the counselors just said that most men she knows masturbate. It's not a problem and Beth should just join in and look at pornography with me and that would probably help our marriage. So obviously we never went back to that counselor."

They finally found a Christian counseling center for sexual addictions, one that helped them on the road to recovery. Unfortunately, in the entire country there are only about three Christian counseling centers that specialize in sexual addictions. "I think it's just a very new field," says Sam. "And up until some of the recent stories in the news with Tiger Woods receiving recovery, it's one of those fields that just isn't talked about a lot. There's so much shame that clouds the whole subject of pornography and sexual addiction. Shame is associated with sexual sin in general and it isn't talked about a lot."

Sam and Beth credit their faith for helping them get through that dark time. Sam says, "Our faith was a big part of never giving up, and I always continued going to priests for confession even though I was really ashamed. I would jump from one priest to another so they wouldn't recognize my voice. But I never gave up on the sacrament of confession. And I think God really answered those prayers by helping us find the counseling centers and some of the other resources, like John Paul II's *Theology of the Body*."

Sam and Beth are now involved with My House Initiative, a freedom-from-pornography program at the Archdiocese of Kansas City in Kansas. Sam runs the My House Initiative office and is also a licensed counselor. He provides counseling in recovery groups for men. Beth coordinates the women's group for the My House Initiative office and, with Sam, gives talks to parishes and groups. Initially, however, Beth was not interested in staying involved with the process.

"Whether I liked it or not, I had developed knowledge through my own experiences with Sam," she says. "And attending a support group and hearing the experiences of other women added to that base of understanding. It was very difficult to say no to helping. My attitude changed from keeping it all inside and not wanting any part of it to wanting to help others. What Sam and I learned from reaching out to help others with this problem became a huge benefit for our own healing as well. So it was very much a blessing."

Sam realizes that most recovery happens because of the women in these men's lives. Sam notes that "80 percent of those men are making that call because of a strong wife or a girlfriend who is advocating for change in the relationship. The reason most of these men call is not because they think it's a good idea. A lot of these men take the first steps toward building a healthy relationship free of pornography only after they're confronted by a strong, loving woman. So I think Beth's ability to encourage and empower the women is just such a gift."

Since she began working with My House Initiative, Beth has received more than one hundred calls from women looking for support and resources to help them deal with the pornography that has invaded their marriages. And when the women have someone to point them in the right direction, she has seen amazing results in their marriages. "The women who stick with it," Beth says, "the women who work on themselves, you see a profound change in them. We still have rough days, but we can turn to each other and help each other through this process. It's not always easy, but coming together and knowing you're not in it by yourself is a good start. And it works."

In 2005 the Archdiocese of Kansas City created an awareness campaign about the effects of pornography and sexual addictions. Six other dioceses have implemented the My House Initiative, and Sam and Beth's hope is that it continues to spread.

Sam and Beth Meier have given emotional presentations and trainings about pornography across the country and have been interviewed by numerous Catholic organizations, including Life on the Rock, FathersForGood.org, and the National Catholic Register. *Sam has a master's degree in counseling, and Beth is enrolled in a graduate theology program at the Maryvale Institute in collaboration with the John Paul II Institute for Studies in Marriage and Family in Rome. They are the proud parents of a one-year-old son and look forward to the day when the majority of Catholics are experiencing more happiness and better intimacy through the beauty of the* Theology of the Body. *To learn more about the My House initiative, go to www.loveisfaithful. com.* | Aired: July 12, 2010

***

Don't Wait, Just Do It

Sixty-seven-year-old Patricia Oetting from Barefoot Bay, Florida, has worked as a nurse for forty-six years. Since October 2008, she has put her skills to use by traveling several times a year to Haiti to work with other medical professionals in the poorest areas of Port-au-Prince. They call their effort The Haiti Clinic.

"It's a group of volunteers, doctors, nurses, and other people," says Patricia. "We all pay our own way. We go into Cité Soleil, which is the largest slum in the Western Hemisphere—three square miles holding three hundred thousand people, with no electricity, no running water, no sanitation, and garbage all over."

The medical team serves as many people as they can during the visits.

"We'll see hundreds of people," says Patricia. "They know ahead of time that we're coming, and they set it up so that we can efficiently take care of the mostly medical issues. There are children with worms—there's such malnutrition there. Everybody has a chronic cough. They all have fevers. They all have acid indigestion: basic problems caused by not eating and by living in a place where's there's charcoal burning all the time. It smells. It gets in your throat."

While in Haiti, Patricia also spends time with the Missionaries of Charity, who have nine convents in Haiti.

"They have a hospital, an orphanage, and a school," she says. "I help with the babies there. You hold them in rocking chairs, you sit, and you love them. You feed them and change their diapers. You're there all day with the wonderful little babies."

Patricia learned of another ministry when she heard Fr. Rick Frechette, who is also a physician, talk about his work in Haiti. He has a ministry called Compassion Weavers, which is dedicated to helping those in the slum areas get an education, clean water, disaster relief, and even something as basic as a dignified burial. Every Thursday, Fr. Rick goes to the morgue and collects the bodies that no one else will bury.

"The people are so poor," Patricia explains, "that not only are they lacking food and water, they don't have any money to bury the bodies of their deceased loved ones, so they have to abandon them. To me that is so sad. That seems like the ultimate poverty—when you can't even bury someone you love."

The death and burial of a loved one is something Patricia understands all too well. When she was eighteen, her own mother died. Her father had no money at the time, and being an only child, Patricia was left with the burden of paying for her mother's funeral.

"I actually had to go to the funeral home and say, 'I have no money to bury my mother. Is there any chance I could pay you five dollars a week and you would bury her?' The man said yes. And it took me three years to pay the bill. I know what it feels like to have no brothers or sisters; it was just me who was responsible for burying someone I loved."

When Patricia is in Haiti, she always finds time to help Fr. Rick bury the dead.

"He has these papier-mâché coffins," says Patricia. "They're the same quality as a Mardi Gras mask. And he pays people to make them, so they're making money. The coffins cost forty-five dollars each. We pay the gravediggers twenty-five dollars each. They have a music band that's there, for fifty dollars. The morgue workers, there are eight of them—they make fifty dollars as a group. We line the coffin with painter's plastic. We place the body in gently, and we put a rosary bead on the head. We cover them with exam paper from a doctor's office and close the coffin and pray for them."

When Patricia is not working as a nurse or traveling to Haiti, she's spending her time at a hospice in her hometown in Florida. Her Catholic faith allows her to view death and dying in a positive light.

"I'm at the hospice every Wednesday from 10:00 in the morning till about 4:30," says Patricia. "I just love being with people who are dying. I think it is a holy moment, such a special time. There's no time for anything but honesty. Some people have family, and I can help with their family. And some people are all alone, so I just sit there and hold their hand. I'm just present to them and praying for them."

For her work with the poor, the ill, and the dying, Patricia draws inspiration from Mother Teresa.

"Mother Teresa once said something like, 'Don't wait for a leader. Do it yourself, person to person.'" she says. "So that's what I'm doing. The ministering of one person to another person is all we're supposed to do in life. If we read Matthew 25, that's what it is. When did you feed the hungry, give drink to the thirsty, clothe the naked, comfort the afflicted, and bury the dead? It's all right there. It's all handed to me. All I have to do is just go do it. It's real easy there in Haiti. They know that I love the Lord, and we do pray and I tell them God loves them. But I don't really preach. But I'm there with them and they know that and I think that's what's important."

Patricia has been to Haiti ten times since she first traveled there in 2008. And she doesn't plan on ending her trips there any time soon.

Patricia Oetting continues her visits to Haiti and helps Fr. Frechette with his Compassion Weavers ministry. When at home she spends her time visiting dying patients at a hospice center and their families, provides respite care for an ailing senior, helps serve the homeless at a soup kitchen, visits and helps homeless people living in the woods, and visits inmates in jail. To help her and Fr. Frechette, go to www.compassionweavers.com. | Aired: January 4, 2010

***
Parched and Redeemed

Heather King has been on a long journey to the Catholic faith and to discovery of her true calling in life. It came after decades of living on the edge and making a lot of wrong turns.

"I have seven brothers and sisters, and I think six of us turned out to have a really bad case of alcoholism and/or drug addiction," Heather says. "Somehow I managed to go to college, graduate from law school, and become a lawyer all while I was drinking, which was quite a feat. I was just a falling-down, blackout drunk. I was a morning drinker, drinking at old-men's bars; this was in Boston. Finally, many years later, I sobered up. I got married, moved to Los Angeles, took the California bar exam, and got a job in Beverly Hills.

"I was getting my drinking under control, but now I had this other big crisis, a spiritual crisis, because I had started to believe in God. I had these big questions. One of the biggest was, 'What are we here for?' I was in such torment trying to figure this out. Not having the answer to this question was worse than the worst days of my drinking. I was so conflicted, thinking, 'This can't be what I'm supposed to do.'"

Heather began to struggle with her career as a lawyer. She became disillusioned with what she saw going on in the justice system and felt she wasn't doing what God wanted her to do. She was feeling the pull to become a full-time writer. She went into a church one day after arguing a case and prayed.

"I sat there and prayed," she says. "I felt real anguish, like Jesus in the garden of Gethsemane. I didn't know what I should do. I so badly wanted to write, but I just didn't dare. I didn't want to be a quitter. I was forty-one years old. I was making money for the first time in my life, and I was sitting there thinking about quitting my job. After much prayer and discernment I eventually found the courage or grace, or whatever you want to call it, to do just that."

During the time Heather felt called to become a full-time writer, she found that she was being drawn more and more to the Catholic Church. "The beginning of my writing and my conversion to Catholicism, going through RCIA and being confirmed, happened almost at the same time," she says.

Heather took a huge leap of faith. She quit her job not knowing where God was leading her but certain that it was the right decision. "I didn't know what I was going to write," she recalled. "I just knew I'd had this calling since I learned to read." Heather became a full-time essayist and memoirist. Her first book, *Parched*, is the story of her twenty years of hardcore alcoholism and how it brought her to a power greater than herself. Her most recent book, *Redeemed*, is the story of her ongoing conversion to Catholicism.

"*Redeemed* is a story of trusting my heart and believing that if I followed this deep, deep call, things would be all right—that there would be enough money, that there would be enough love, and that this was really supposed to be my contribution to the world," says Heather. "I think that's one of the desert journeys that a lot of people are stuck in, often for their whole lives. It's the journey to find meaningful work, work that we're passionate about. When you're doing work you love, you don't care that you don't have a ton of money. You're just happy to know that your life is rich in other ways."

Heather has been able to support herself by writing books and essays and as an occasional commentator on NPR's show *All Things Considered*. Heather is living out her faith with words so others might come to know what she's discovered about it. She says, "I think we need stories, we need paintings, we need music to move our hearts and open our hearts. We need to turn our hearts from stone to flesh and come to this unbelievable person of Christ."

Heather relates a chapter from *Redeemed* to Christ and the Advent season we celebrate each year. She sees how her own journey coincides with that of the Christ Child. "The last passage in *Redeemed* is about the fact that we spend so much of our lives waiting. And again, the waiting is kind of a cross, and then in an odd way it's also a blessing because there can be a real fullness in the waiting, just like a woman when she's bearing a baby.

"I think you could meditate forever on the fact that Christ came into the world as a child. It makes me cry that God would send the smallest, most hidden, most anonymous, vulnerable form of a human being to come into the world to be our savior. But it's how he moves our hearts. It's how he reveals himself in our day. It's vulnerability. That's a beautiful lesson at Christmas and a beautiful time to come back to the table and rejoin the human race."

Heather King is an ex-lawyer, sober alcoholic, contemplative, and Catholic convert who lives in Los Angeles. She is the author of two memoirs, Parched *and* Redeemed: A Spiritual Misfit Stumbles Toward God, Marginal Sanity, and the Peace That Passes All Understanding. *Her newest book is* Shirt of Flame: A Year with Saint Thérèse of Lisieux. *Visit her website at www.heather-king.com. She blogs at shirtofflame.blogspot.com.* | *Aired: December 15, 2008*

* * *

MOVED TO ACTION: QUESTIONS FOR THOUGHT

1. Tim Jaccard could have been swallowed up in despair after having seen so many babies die. Instead, he took action. Has there been a time in your own life when God was calling you to take action on something? Did you respond? If not, why?
2. In the midst of despair over losing her friend Fr. Mychal Judge, Kelly Ann Lynch was able to hear a calling from God. When you are in the midst of sorrow, are you able to hear God's promptings in your life? Who helps you get through the hard times?
3. Have you or someone you know struggled with pornography? After hearing Sam and Beth Meier's story, do you think differently about this addiction? Do you understand how this affects more than just the person viewing the pornography? What can you do to make sure this doesn't come into your life or that of someone you love?
4. On a daily basis, Patricia Oetting puts herself in the presence of death and dying. She relies on her faith to give her strength. Do you know any individuals, either sick or dying, who could use your comforting presence in their lives? How could you turn their despair into hope?
5. Heather King struggled with alcoholism for many years. Have you or someone you love struggled with an addiction? Were you able to support them or yourself by turning to God?

CHAPTER | TWO |

THE PLIGHT OF JOB
Remaining Faithful Against All Odds

Then Job arose, tore his robe, shaved his head, and fell on the ground and worshiped. He said, "Naked I came from my mother's womb, and naked shall I return there; the LORD gave, and the LORD has taken away; blessed be the name of the LORD."
—Job 1:20–21

SURVIVOR'S GUILT

Michael Nolte has experienced the kind of tragedy that most of us are never called on to endure. And the random accident that nearly took his life, far from shaking his faith or leaving him depressed, seems instead to have sharpened his spirit and left him suffused with joy.

On May 22, 2003, Michael, a small-business owner living in Leawood, Kansas, was driving to Missouri to help make funeral arrangements for a family friend when he was pulled over by Missouri Patrol Trooper Michael Newton, to receive a warning for driving too long in the left lane. Officer Newton asked Michael to join him in the patrol car while he wrote up the citation. While they were sitting in the front seat of the cruiser, a one-ton truck veered from the road and struck the back of the car at 65 mph. In less than two seconds, the cruiser was engulfed in flames.

Two passing motorists stopped and tried to help the men out of the car. They managed to pull Michael out, but they couldn't reach Officer Newton, and he perished in the accident. "The Good Samaritans had come to the passenger side, not the driver side," Michael recalls. "The amount of time they had to pull somebody out, through the car window, was fifteen seconds. And they pulled me." As a result of this chance rescue, Michael suffered from survivor's guilt for a long time. "I felt very guilty for being alive and for Officer Newton being dead."

Doctors later told Michael that he came within fifteen seconds of burning to death. He suffered third-degree burns over 40 percent of his body. His hair and eyebrows were gone, his face and neck burned, his left ear melted, his left hand burned to the bone and, worst of all, he was badly burned from his feet to just above his knees, along with the soles of his feet.

Michael spent two and a half months in the hospital, in an intensive-care burn-treatment unit, going through the most excruciating pain he had ever known. The removal of dead skin and skin grafts occurred about every other day. Even the maximum dosage of pain medicine didn't seem to help. His parish priest at the time, Fr. Al Rockers, was a source of strength for Michael. "Fr. Al would call a couple times a week," Michael says. "One time he asked me if the pain was excruciating. I thought I could admit the truth to him: I told him it hurt so bad that I couldn't even pray, and I felt bad about that. Father told me that until my pain had lessened, I shouldn't flog myself because I couldn't pray. Instead, he said, I should offer up my pain as my prayer. That was a very affirming thing to hear, and it gave me such relief."

With the help of his wife, his three daughters, and the larger community, Michael returned home and started life again. He still has to deal with constant pain, but through therapy and time, he is now able to walk short distances and dress himself, and he has been able to return to a job that he loves. He can now work part-time for the company he founded, Nolte's Bridal Selections.

Michael doesn't blame God for what happened. In fact, he feels that God gave him this extraordinary experience in order to draw other people closer to Him. "It's taken me two years to be able to talk about it without breaking down," he says. But talking about it is key. "If I just insist on keeping it in a locked box it doesn't do anybody any good."

"I had a long way to go in terms of really understanding what role Jesus played in my life," Michael says. "And a long way to go in understanding what Jesus did for me when he submitted his body to the torture of scourging and being on the cross. I did not understand that level of pain until I was a burn victim."

Michael doesn't complain about the physical suffering he still endures every day. He is completely focused on the future. "I have never asked God why he allowed this to happen to me," he says. "But I did ask him why he spared me. I have come to believe that everything that's happened in my life has helped to prepare me for this launching pad and that now the purpose of my life is much more clearly defined. These experiences—being pulled from a burning car, living through the hell of burn-care treatment—these were the defining experiences that made me who I was supposed to be, and I am determined to take this experience and turn it into good for somebody else."

Michael has done just that. He established a scholarship fund for Officer Newton's son, who was five years old at the time of the accident.

He also set up scholarship money for the daughters of his lifesavers, a total of five children who are benefiting from his generosity. He continues to give to others and is quick to point out that he didn't get through this ordeal by himself.

"We had a tremendous amount of support from our parish family and our neighborhood," says Michael. "I would get notification that I was on a prayer chain for a Lutheran church in Iowa or a Methodist church in Nebraska or a Baptist church out in Colorado. And that kind of combined prayer I really believe is what pulled me through it. I could physically feel it when people were praying for me. My faith has helped me because it makes sense of all that's happened to me. I know about depression. I know about survivor's guilt. And I would have never had the privilege of walking a mile in those shoes if I had not lived through this wreck."

Michael's use of the word *privilege* to describe the pain and suffering he has been through is indicative of his attitude and his astounding faith. As he continues to face his daily struggle, Michael is an inspiration. And he's on a mission: "I will go wherever somebody needs to hear this story, because God spared my life for some reason. And I think a part of it is to just tell the story of the miracle of many people and how they worked together. I just love being alive. Nobody has a better life than Mike Nolte."

Michael Nolte is a successful business owner with two couture bridal salons in Kansas City. He is the author of Burned But Not Broken: For What Was I Spared? *and a speaker. He has been married to Barbie for thirty-one years and is the father of three daughters. As a result of the wreck, Congress enacted the Pass With Care law requiring motorists to move over when they see flashing lights on the shoulder, thus preventing untold numbers of similar tragedies.* | *Aired: April 3, 2006*

***
Jesus, Save Us!

Robert Rogers seemed to have it all: a beautiful loving wife, Melissa, and four wonderful children. Their lives were challenging at times—one of their sons had been born with Down syndrome—but despite that, after having three of their own children, Robert and Melissa felt called to adopt a special-needs girl from China. Their lives in Kansas were full, and their family and their faith were always first and foremost in their lives.

Then one day in August 2003, while driving home from a wedding in Wichita, in a matter of seconds, right before his eyes, Robert lost his entire family. Nine inches of rain fell in a six-hour period that day; the Rogers family was caught in the downpour and swept up in flooding on the highway. More than 32,000 gallons of water were rushing over the freeway every second, and it overtook the Rogerses' van so quickly there was no way they could get out with their four small children. They instantly turned to prayer.

"In the van we sought the Lord," Robert says. "We were saying, 'Jesus save us, Jesus save us.' And he truly did."

Amid the terror and fear, Robert says, the Lord filled the van with peace.

"I just had a peace that somehow we were going to be OK. The water would go back down and we'd be all right. But it didn't do that. So we were saying, 'Jesus,' and we were singing praises and saying Scripture. Psalm 46 came to my lips. It says, 'God is our strength, God is our refuge, an ever present help in times of trouble.' I think it's so important to memorize Scripture, because you never know when you're going to need it."

Eventually, Robert was able to break open the window, but when he did, he, Melissa, and their oldest daughter, Makenah, were sucked out of the car. The three younger children remained in the van in their car seats. That was the last time Robert saw his family alive.

"It was as if the hand of God was there just lifting us up to heaven," says Robert. "I can't explain it other than that. God was there in the waters. And even though my family's bodies drowned, they did not perish. I know they are in heaven, because we had Jesus in our hearts. I kissed death. I collapsed over each one of their bodies when I had to identify them and cried like a baby. And I still cry all the time. But I can tell you that the grave has no victory. Death has no sting. The grief stung. The grief was horribly painful and still is. But I just knew death didn't win. I knew right where they were."

Most people would have given up on God after such a tragedy, but Robert chose trust over despair, and he carried on.

"I made a choice," he says. "I made a choice to trust God. I made a choice not to be bitter, but to be better. I had every reason in the world to be bitter. We'd been through two excruciating miscarriages, through Down syndrome, through the adoption process, had two special-needs kids, an orphan, all these trials in life. And yet God still ushered my family to heaven when we cried out to Him to save us.

"It was too catastrophic and huge to believe that God's hand wasn't somehow in it. I didn't know how I wasn't blaming God. I just said, 'God, this is bigger than any of us. It's clear you are going to use this for the glory, and I'm going to allow you to do that.' And it's been a choice. That's all I can say. I've chosen to surrender my family from the moment I identified them. The times that I thought I would be the weakest, truly God has been the strongest through me. This past year and a half has been the richest time with God in my whole life, because I have chosen to be consumed by Him and not by the things of this world. I just see that I'm alive by a miracle and God has a purpose for my life and I don't want to blow it.

"Psalm 139 says, 'All of our days are ordained and written in His book before one of them came to be.' And so God knows. He knew the moment of our birth, the moment of our death. And I just have to believe that my family did everything on this earth they were supposed to do. And now they're still touching lives through me as a broken vessel, as an instrument. I'm just honored to be an instrument of peace and an instrument of God's work to touch lives."

Robert's advice for those seeking a closer relationship with the Lord: "Start living a life of no regrets today, because you can get right with God, right now."

Robert Rogers, author of Into the Deep: One Man's Story of How Tragedy Took His Family but Could Not Take His Faith, *is an electrical engineer and accomplished songwriter and pianist. He resigned from his technical career in 2004 to form Mighty in the Land Ministry. He freely shares his testimony of "no regrets" around the world and calls Fort Wayne, Indiana, his home. Find his ministry at www.mightyintheland.com. | Aired: April 20, 2005*

***

A SILENT KILLER

By the looks of things, John and Patricia Gallagher had an ideal life. They had four beautiful children, a nice home in the suburbs, and a good marriage. Trisha and her kids were even featured on *The Oprah Winfrey Show* twice. Trisha had written a book called *Raising Happy Kids on a Reasonable Budget*.

"Everything was fine," Trisha recalls. "We had a happy marriage—not that we didn't have a few marriage-counseling sessions here and there over the years. John went to work and I was at home with the kids. I did some part-time things. I was writing books and doing that kind of thing."

In 1999, the Gallaghers' world began to fall apart. John told Trisha his company was downsizing and he was going to need to look for another job. Trisha began to notice changes in John.

"He was losing weight," she says. "And he wasn't sleeping. Sometimes he'd think he was choking on chicken, and we would go to the hospital and there would be no chicken, or we'd be at the mall and he'd think he was having a heart attack. This was very different behavior for him. But we didn't know that these were the signs of male depression: irritability, lack of sleep, all the classic signs. John wasn't acting the same, but we were all trying to act like there was nothing wrong."

John spent thirteen stressful months searching for another job, and his symptoms persisted. "During those thirteen months we were sure he had a brain tumor or stomach ulcers, so we were going to every medical doctor," says Trish. "John went to thirty-four doctor appointments during that year because we were sure there was a physical ailment; we never even thought of the word *depression*."

On April 28, 1999, Trisha's world would change dramatically. She awoke to find her husband standing beside the bed. John looked down at her and said, "Trisha, I tried to kill myself. I went to the bridge but I couldn't do it." He told her he had also ingested carbon monoxide. Trisha took him to the hospital immediately.

John was initially sent home from the hospital. They returned a few days later because he was having blood-pressure problems, but the hospital was not going to admit him for psychological care. While John was alone in his room, he took matters into his own hands. He jumped out the window from the cardiac floor.

"He fell forty-five feet into a cement viaduct" and survived, Trisha says.

After the suicide attempt, Trisha turned the house upside down, looking for clues to help her make sense of the situation. "I cleaned out everything," she says. "I was cleaning out clothes for Goodwill. I was tearing the house apart. I was going through his briefcases, his drawers, his pockets. I was so sure that I was going to find some evidence that he was having an affair, that he had a baby with somebody else. I didn't have any reason to believe that. But what I found were different referrals from his primary-care physician—a few of them, for him to get psychiatric care."

John's legs were crushed in the fall, but with therapy he eventually was able to walk again. For many years, John and Trisha chose not to tell anyone the reason for his injuries. They felt embarrassed and confused, so they told people that John had been in a car accident. The strain took its toll on the whole family. After a year and a half, John and Trisha separated for five years.

"When this happened, in the beginning," says Trisha, "I wanted to wheel John into every Catholic parish and say to every woman out there: If your husband isn't eating, isn't sleeping, is irritable, has lost weight, doesn't want to play his guitar, won't go to the zoo, isn't appreciative of his Father's Day gifts, these are signs of depression. I really feel that if I had known these things, it wouldn't have happened."

After years of remaining silent about their situation, John was finally convinced he needed to speak out. He read a story about a seventeen-year-old boy in a neighboring town who had jumped nine floors from his apartment building and survived. John felt he had to do something. He told Trisha he wanted to write a book, and he had a plan.

Trisha recalls: "He said he wanted me to call the girls home from college and he wanted them each to write a chapter." Together, the Gallaghers wrote the book *No More Secrets: A Family Speaks Out About Depression, Anxiety, and Attempted Suicide*. Each member of the family wrote a chapter about how they were affected by John's mental illness. The healing process began when they were able to finally understand each other's experiences. John and Trisha now speak, on average, three times a week at different churches and organizations. The book project and their candor with respect to the issue has helped them come back together and heal. Their Catholic faith has also helped sustain them over these long years of coping.

"I would honestly say that my faith and John's really grew," Trisha says.

Suicide is the eleventh leading cause of death in this country. More than thirty thousand people die from suicide every year. The Gallaghers are working hard to make sure those statistics are lowered.

"There is a message that has to get out there for women, for men, and about how kids are affected when a parent is depressed," says Trisha. "John says, 'It may sound like a cliché, but if I can help one other person not have to go through the turmoil I put my family through, then my coming out to share has been worth it.'"

John and Trisha have come a long way together, but it hasn't been a fairy-tale ending. They're still working on their marriage and working on getting the message out to others about depression. But they're confident now that their faith in God and in each other will sustain them for the long journey ahead.

Patricia Gallagher is the author of seven books and the creator of the Team of Angels pins. When Patricia's children were young, before depression touched her family, she appeared as a guest on CNN, The Early Show *on CBS,* The Oprah Winfrey Show, *and elsewhere. She welcomes speaking engagements to help other families who are experiencing similar circumstances. She can be reached at www.patriciausa.com. | Aired: August 19, 2009*

***

CHOOSE TO PICK UP YOUR CROSS

The amazing thing about forty-one-year-old John Foppe is not that he flies around the world giving motivational talks, or that he's a life coach, or an author, or a devoted husband and friend. It's not even that John does all this without having any arms. The amazing thing about John Foppe is his attitude and his faith.

Born without arms, John uses his feet for most of the day-to-day tasks that other people usually rely on their hands for.

"I drive a car with my feet," he says, "but I don't have special equipment on it. My right foot operates the gas and the brake pedals, and my left foot operates the steering wheel. I also dress myself in the morning. I have a full-length mirror on the wall in the bedroom so I can sit down on the floor; I hold a brush with my toes or maybe an electric razor with my feet, so I can bring my foot up to my face. I also cook. I have a tall bar stool in the kitchen that I sit on; it gets me about level with the countertop or the cooktop, and it frees me up to use both my feet."

Beyond attending to the daily necessities of taking care of himself, John is also an artist, using his feet as hands to create watercolor paintings. Some in John's situation might be preoccupied with learning the cause of their circumstances, but John says he has no desire to find out what caused him to be born without arms.

"I don't really care to know," he says. "I don't know what it would change, and I think it's more important to look at the 'what' in life. You know, *what* do you have control over? What direction do you need to be heading in today? The 'why' question can quickly suck you into a dead-end road of self pity."

Through the tough love of his parents, John learned early that whatever he wanted to make of his life was up to him. He was going to have to choose what to do with the cross he'd been given.

"Yes, it's a cross to bear," he says, "but where I'd draw the distinction is, Jesus tells us to pick up our cross and follow him. So when I talk about a choice, it's really choosing to pick it up."

People sometimes ask John if he would change his situation if he could. "I say no, not anymore," he says. "I chose to pick up the cross. Is it easy? No. But I think it's made me a better person, it has made me a stronger person. And there comes a point where you can have the condition, or the condition can have you. It doesn't have to be a cross of victimhood."

John was quick to point out that he is not alone in his life. He enjoys the support of a helpful network of friends and family—people like his wife and others he can talk to about his frustrations. And then there's his faith.

"My faith plays an incredible role in helping me understand the redemptive value of suffering," John says. "I don't know if other religions have that or if it comes across as clearly for them, but I think that as Catholic Christians we find an incredible spirituality in the notion of physical suffering."

John demonstrates his faith every day to the people he meets. His book *What's Your Excuse? Making the Most of What You Have* is just one of the ways he shares what he has learned. And he doesn't want to stop sharing his good news.

"I help people live their lives fully," he says. "My mission is to redefine human ability. A full life is possible even with a lot of limitations. I've seen this world that God has created for us; it's an awesome world and there's just an awesome life out there. People don't always have a choice in what they're going to do today. They don't always have a choice in where they're going to go today. But I believe all human beings have a choice as to who they're going to be today."

John Foppe is married and has a beautiful four-year-old daughter. From 2008 to 2011 he served as executive director of Community Link, a multimillion-dollar nonprofit agency that through one hundred companies serves more than four hundred people with developmental disabilities. He continues to travel the world, working with organizations to help motivate people through tough times. | Aired: November 28, 2005

** *

Moved to Action: Questions for Thought

1. Job suffered much mental and physical anguish, knowing that his family and possessions were being taken away from him. Michael Nolte will experience chronic pain for the rest of his life. Have you ever experienced intense or chronic physical pain? How did you respond? What can you take from Michael's experience to apply to your own life?
2. Like Job, Robert Rogers had his entire family taken away from him in an instant. Have you ever felt that something was taken unexpectedly from your own life? A child? A relationship? A career? How did you react? Whom did you look to for comfort?
3. What have you learned from Patricia Gallagher and her family? Do you know anyone who has attempted suicide? Have you ever been depressed? Do you think you would turn to God and your faith if you were presented with this situation? Would you be able to praise God for it as Job did?
4. Job could have cursed God for his misfortune, but instead he praised Him. John Foppe could have asked, "Why me? Why was I born without arms?" but he didn't. Is there something in your own life that you haven't fully accepted and still blame God for? What can you do to change that?

CHAPTER | THREE |

THE CONVERSION OF SAUL
Finding a Home in the Church

So Ananias went and entered the house. He laid his hands on Saul and said, "Brother Saul, the Lord Jesus, who appeared to you on your way here, has sent me so that you may regain your sight and be filled with the Holy Spirit." And immediately something like scales fell from his eyes, and his sight was restored. Then he got up and was baptized, and after taking some food, he regained his strength.

—Acts 9:17–19

SMART PEOPLE DON'T BELIEVE IN GOD

Many of us who grew up Catholic and attended Catholic schools in America might have made it all the way to adulthood without encountering anyone who even remotely resembled an atheist. And there are others, of course, who may have had just the opposite sort of upbringing. Jennifer Fulwiler, a former atheist from Austin, Texas, never imagined that she might end up a happy Catholic.

"An atheist is someone who's sure," says Jennifer. "When I was an atheist, I was sure there was no God. It just seemed quite plainly obvious to me. I never once remember, even as a child, even considering the notion that there could be a God. We didn't have a religious family, and I've never been to church with both of my parents."

Jennifer was not just a passive atheist; she took steps to ensure that her beliefs would stay intact. She had specific criteria she adhered to even when looking for a husband.

"I wanted him to be smart, to have a good sense of humor, and he couldn't believe in God," she says. Jennifer found someone whom she thought met those requirements.

"My husband wasn't very religious, and he was very smart. And I assumed that, of course, smart people don't believe in God. Eventually, though, it came out that he, in fact, had a very firm belief in God, and I just couldn't quite seem to talk him out of it. He had grown up very poor and ended up with degrees from Yale, Columbia, and Stanford, so there was no denying he was a very smart guy, yet he believed in God. My old belief about all smart people being atheists didn't work any more after I'd met my husband."

Jennifer's husband didn't practice his Christianity in any formal way, but he did hold to his belief in God. Besides that, in 2004 there was another event that made Jennifer rethink her atheism.

"I was twenty-seven, and I had my first child," she says. "I was still an atheist, but I had this sense that I wanted to make sure I was right. For the first time I was willing to set my pride aside and just admit that I wanted to know the truth. If I was going to teach my child that God does not exist, I wanted to make sure I had it right."

Since her husband had been raised Baptist, they entertained the possibility of Christianity, but becoming Catholic was still not on the radar.

"I remember joking one time with another couple at dinner," Jennifer recalls. "We said that we were exploring different religions, and that Christianity could be a possibility. But we made a joke that, obviously, it wouldn't be Catholic Christianity; it was going to be something more reasonable."

And so Jennifer embarked on her research. But she didn't proceed in a traditional way.

"I started looking around and realized that we simply did not know any religious people," she says. "This was back in late summer of 2005, and I thought, well, maybe there are some Christians on the Internet. So I started a blog, and I encouraged people to leave comments. I began visiting atheist sites and Christian sites and watching the debates that would go on between atheists and Christians.

"Looking back, I see that was very clearly the hand of God in my life, because I don't think that I would be Catholic, maybe not even Christian yet at this point, if it weren't for starting a blog. I'd stretch my mind to ask the most difficult questions, and it was the Catholics who had very compelling answers."

"After a while of praying, reading the Bible, and visiting some churches, I felt like I had some conclusions. But obviously I wasn't going to become *Catholic*. I mean, the Catholic Church is weird and antiquated and sometimes the people in it do seriously bad stuff. But I was interested to at least explore this line of thinking and see what I found. Reading the *Catechism of the Catholic Church* was like nothing I'd ever experienced. This was truth. I knew it. I'd finally found it. It described God, our relationship to him, the Bible, Jesus, moral truths—the entire human experience—in a way that resonated on a deep level."

Jennifer and her husband entered the Catholic Church in 2007 at the Easter Vigil and settled in at St. William parish in Round Rock, Texas. But Jennifer wasn't about to be quiet about her newfound faith.

"I often ask some of my Catholic friends, some who maybe don't go to church or who are not that into their faith, 'Do you believe in God?' They'll say yes, and I then ask them, 'Why doesn't your life revolve around that? Why isn't every aspect of your life informed by that belief?'

"I think some Catholics might be a little bit afraid to scratch the surface of their faith. Maybe a little bit afraid to ask the tough questions because they're kind of afraid of what they might find. And one of the things I'm just shouting from the rooftops about it is, *Ask the tough questions!* Explore your faith, because as a Catholic, you will only be led to discover the immense knowledge and beauty of the Catholic Church, and you will only grow deeper in your faith by asking every tough question that comes to mind."

In addition to her blogging and Internet explorations, Jennifer also learned a lot by reading books written by Catholics.

"I just can't encourage Catholics enough to read the great Catholic writers," she advises. "Read the people from previous time periods, such as St. Thomas Aquinas, St. Francis de Sales, and G.K. Chesterton, and read the modern writers such as Scott Hahn and Mark Shea, both of whom are converts. There is a wealth of information just from the Catholic authors alone, and you can really, really deepen your faith by picking up some of their books. Given my background, I would say to cradle Catholics or maybe even to converts who converted many years ago, 'You have a lot to be excited about here. You can't even imagine the gold mine that you are sitting on.'"

Jennifer Fulwiler has been married for seven years and lives in Austin, Texas, with her husband and five children. When she's not busy with her job of managing the chaos of her busy household, she does freelance writing and is working on a memoir about her conversion. She is also a blogger for the National Catholic Register. | *Aired: March 3, 2008*

***
Prison Time Is Thinking Time

Joseph Pearce is a respected writer-in-residence and an associate professor of literature at Ave Maria University in Naples, Florida. But to hear the circumstances of his upbringing and youth, you would find it hard to believe he ended up where he is. He was born in the early 1960s on the outskirts of London.

"It was a period of large-scale immigration to England," Joseph says. "In the area where I was growing up, the immigrants were largely from Pakistan and India. And there was a great deal of tension between the indigenous white population and these new arrivals. As an angry teenager I got swept up into all of that. Consequently, by the age of fifteen, I had become involved with a white-supremacist, racist organization called the National Front."

Joseph had been baptized in the Anglican church, but his family never participated in any church, and talk of God was a nonissue in his home. He was about as far away from the Catholic Church as one could get.

"I was already inclined against Catholicism," he says, "but then when I got involved in the politics of Northern Ireland and joined the Orange Order, which is a Protestant secret society, and then got involved with the Ulster Defense Association and the Ulster Volunteer Force, which were paramilitary terrorist groups—this obviously hardened my anti-Catholicism still further."

"Violence was just part of the scene, part of the whole culture and atmosphere in which I lived. I was never someone who looked for or enjoyed violence. On the contrary, if I could avoid it I would. But it was part of the air that I breathed. I was involved in street brawls and have the scars to show for it. I was certainly more than happy to defend myself in the violent milieu in which I found myself."

Joseph was a skilled writer at an early age, and at sixteen he put his talents to work by writing for newspapers that fueled the prejudices he held. In 1982, after being involved in these extremist politics for several years, he was arrested.

"I went to prison twice for the same offense, which was publishing material likely to incite racial hatred," he explains. "It was for editing a youth magazine called *Bulldog*, a newspaper of the Young National Front. It was a virulent, violent journal that aimed at stirring up hatred between the races. The first time I went to prison, I was very, very militant, and I considered myself to be a political prisoner."

Joseph was sent to prison again four years later, but this time, while he was doing his time, his attitude began to change. He was beginning to doubt his devotion to the cause. Since he had always been an avid reader, he was familiar with some Catholic writers, and some of their ideas began to take root.

"I had been reading Catholic materials for quite some time," he recalls, "and there was this struggle going on in my heart and head between these hardened political and racial and bigoted ideas and these new Christian ideas. I first started reading Catholic writers when I was only about nineteen, when I was an absolute fanatic. And of course I wasn't interested in their Catholicism. On the contrary, I was opposed to their Catholicism, but I was interested in some of their political ideas. Through Chesterton, I was introduced to his friend Belloc and then John Henry Newman and C.S. Lewis and J.R.R. Tolkien. Once you start reading all of these people, these great Catholic and Christian thinkers, there is this intellectual enlightenment that goes on and also this deeper healing that happens at the same time."

"By the time I went to prison the second time, I had been reading these authors for several years, and the Catholic ideas were sufficiently powerful that I had severe doubts about my political beliefs. The prison sentence happened in the middle of this conversion process. During this second sentence in prison, somebody sent me some rosary beads. I actually wanted to pray them. But of course this was impossible because I didn't know the Hail Mary or the Glory Be or the Creed. What I did was to start mumbling sort of inarticulate prayers and fumbling my way around the beads and praying. This was the beginning of my prayer life. And that coincided with a flood of grace and answers pouring in and a great desire to become a Catholic. And in prison I started going to Mass for the first time."

Joseph was received into the Church in 1989. He was a full-time writer for several years in England, and then in 2001 accepted the position he has with Ave Maria University in Florida. He continues to teach and write, only this time he's not inciting passion for hatred, he's teaching a passion for beauty and good.

"To become a Catholic is to come home, absolutely," Joseph says. "That's exactly what I feel. And it's the greatest gift one can possibly receive. The greatest moment in my life was my reception into the Church."

Joseph Pearce, writer-in-residence and associate professor of literature at Ave Maria University, is the author of many books on Shakespeare and Catholic literary figures, including J.R.R. Tolkien, G.K. Chesterton, and Oscar Wilde. | Aired: March 15, 2010

* * *

MULTIPLE MIRACLES

Most people would say that they haven't experienced one true miracle in their life. But Kari Beckman, from Atlanta, would say that God sent her not just one miracle but three. Kari grew up in an unstable, mostly nonreligious atmosphere troubled by divorce, chronic poverty, and a painful medical condition.

"Growing up in a very dysfunctional background, when things got tough I would be handed off, sent to a foster person or a friend or a cousin, or to someone else in the family," she says.

At the age of sixteen, Kari was ready to emancipate herself from her family, drop out of high school, and get on with life on her own. But one of her teachers, Mrs. Aston, had other plans. She didn't let Kari drop out and instead took great interest in Kari's talents and potential.

"Mrs. Aston took me on as her special project," says Kari. "So I would spend the weekends at her house (of course, now teachers would be fired for that). She really became my mother. And part of being at her house was the fact that she was Catholic, and we would go to Saturday night Mass every weekend. She was an amazing woman who, because of the way she lived out her faith, just really loved me in a way I had never been loved before. So she was my first miracle."

Kari eventually joined the Catholic Church, with Mrs. Aston standing by her side as her godmother. But her passion for the faith waned for a while, until she and her husband had to move to a new town for his job. They knew no one, and Kari looked to the church to meet new people.

"In the church bulletin it said, 'Life in the Eucharist Seminar,'" she recalls. "You should understand that I had no idea what *Eucharist* meant, and I was never instructed on the true presence of Our Lord."

Kari went to the seminar, and because she hadn't been well catechized, she was surprised to learn about the Church's teachings on fertility, contraception, confession, and the Eucharist. She'd never been to eucharistic adoration and had no idea what it was.

"The next thing I know, a man in a funny cape comes in with a beautiful gold object in his hands and everyone starts singing," Kari says. "And when he held up the monstrance and it stopped right in front of me, I just started crying. I had no idea what was happening to me. And I cried for three days straight, even in my sleep, the tears continued. And of course later I would find out that that's the gift of tears. A lot of times when you come to the Lord, He uses that just to cleanse you."

Kari's gift of tears was her second miracle. After her experience with the seminar, she and her husband decided not to practice contraception and to be open to life. They had already had one child, but owing to Kari's medical condition, that pregnancy had been difficult and dangerous both for her son and for Kari.

"I was born with a condition called a complete uterus didelphys, which is two uteruses and two cervixes," Kari explains. "Most women with that condition don't have any live children; they miscarry them. We went to a surgeon, because I was having more complications, and we weren't going to use contraception, and we would certainly welcome children, but we weren't sure that I could do that. They went in to do surgery on me and they found that I was completely normal now on the inside."

Knowing Kari's history and medical problems, the doctor who did her surgery was amazed at what he now found. He researched his findings overnight and then spoke with Kari and her husband the next morning.

Kari remembers the moment: "That morning he walked into my hospital room, put in the videotape, and showed us. 'You have one uterus and one cervix,' he said. And he said, 'Ma'am, I don't know what you believe in, but I believe in God and I can't explain this. This is one of those medical things that are beyond our hands.'"

Kari's third miracle brought her closer to God and deepened her faith. And now she and her husband are blessed to be raising eight beautiful children.

Kari Beckman is the founder and director of Regina Caeli Academy in Norcross and Fayetteville, Georgia. Regina Caeli is a Christ-centered academy where the daily life of the teachers and students revolves around and is permeated by the teachings of Jesus Christ. They have one hundred thirty students on two campuses. | Aired: March 22, 2010

Death of the Innocents

Steven Mosher, from Front Royal, Virginia, made a long journey from his early days of relativistic beliefs to find his way to the Catholic faith. He was raised with the secular belief that morals were all relative and ethics were situational—that you could do whatever you wanted, depending on the circumstances, and that any action could be justified because there were no absolute standards in morality.

Steven was attending Stanford University when his long-held beliefs began to be challenged.

"I was in the anthropology department at Stanford University when China opened up to the West in 1979," Steven explains. "I'm a cultural anthropologist by training, and I was privileged to be the first American social scientist selected to go to China. I can speak, read, and write Chinese—in fact, several dialects of Chinese—and I went there with no particular religious beliefs. One of the beliefs I did hold was that China was overpopulated. Another thing I believed was that the Chinese Communist party had done wonderful things for workers and peasants."

During the time Steven spent in China, he found that his preconceived ideas were not in fact true.

"I was there for a year, long enough for people to tell me that, no, it wasn't so, that China's problem was too much government. That was a real eye-opening experience."

The event that really solidified the change in Steven's belief system was when he witnessed China's one-child-per-family policy go into effect.

"I was working in a village when the one-child policy began," Steven says. "I saw women arrested for the crime, the supposed crime of being pregnant. Because pregnancy, at least pregnancy with a second or third or fourth child, had been declared a crime against the state. My conversion really began when I witnessed a cesarean-section abortion on a woman who was seven-and-a-half months pregnant. I saw with my own eyes what an abortion really was, and it was the death of an innocent human being and the deep wounding of the mother. I began to seek an explanation as to why such great evil could happen. So I began to seek the good, and if you seek the good you will eventually be led to God."

Steven returned to Stanford and wrote about the population-control horrors he had witnessed. Bowing to demands of the Chinese government, Stanford actually expelled Steven rather than grant him the Ph.D. he had earned. He even went to speak with representatives from the National Organization for Women, hoping they would help him in exposing this harmful policy.

"I was surprised to find out they weren't interested in helping," says Steven. "They talk a lot about being committed to choice, but they weren't willing to fight for the right of Chinese women to choose to have children."

Steven committed himself to the pro-life cause and through that was drawn to the Catholic faith. In 1991 he came into full communion with the Catholic Church. And in 1995 he became president of the Population Research Institute in Virginia.

"We've been fairly successful in arguing that our foreign aid, for example, should be going into primary health-care programs and programs that build roads and save lives instead of into programs that promote abortion, sterilization, and contraception overseas," he says. "We've been arguing that the UN Population Fund should respect the rights of couples to decide for themselves the number and spacing of their children. We've been fighting against forced-sterilization campaigns in Latin America, in Indonesia, in India, and in other places."

The fight to dispel the myth of overpopulation is not an easy one, but Steven and his colleagues at the Population Research Institute are not going to give up.

"Part of our work is education, and we've got a lot of material up on our website at pop.org, including some very interesting short YouTube videos that make clear the points I've been talking about. I know we've been effective. We've been able to pass laws against the worst kind of abuses. But the fight continues and I'm glad to be a part of it."

We should all be glad, too, that Steven is a part of the fight.

Steven Mosher is president of the Population Research Institute and the author of a number of books on China. He has served as director of the Asian Studies Center at the Claremont Institute and as commissioner of the U.S. Commission on Broadcasting to the PRC. He is frequently invited to address the intelligence community on national-security matters. | Aired: March 29, 2010

***

My Guru Mentor

Tucker Coon, who attends a parish in Naples, Florida, has had quite an interesting journey to the Catholic Church. Tuck, as most people call him, recounts his early days growing up: "My parents never went to church, and by the time I got to college I thought I was an atheist and I guess I was. And then after my divorce in Australia in 1980, I was looking for some sort of a refuge, some place I could go to for spiritual support."

Interestingly enough, Tuck found some wisdom at his local YMCA in Australia. He says, "This lady at the Y, an old lady who looked remarkably like Mother Teresa, suggested I go to the Siddha Yoga ashram in Melbourne, Australia."

Tuck moved into the ashram, which is a communal house whose members share spiritual goals and practices such as yoga or other Hindu disciplines. Tuck began studying Siddha Yoga. According to Tuck, "In Siddha Yoga, the guru, by touch, word, or thought, awakens God within you."

Tuck continued working at his day job while living and learning at the ashram. He worked at an advertising agency, writing car ads for General Motors. Tuck says, "It was a tremendous back-and-forth. It was like being on a rubber band between the totally spiritual—sitting in a room full of incense and chanting and watching talks by Baba and other experts from India—and then going to the advertising agency and dealing with account executives and clients and television producers. It was a tremendous exercise, managing the tension between the world and the spirit."

Tuck's guru mentor from Australia moved to Los Angeles, and Tuck followed and stayed there for a while. "I lived at the ashram for a couple of years before I came to Naples in 2003," he says. "And I realized I had learned everything that the ashram could teach."

Once in Naples, Tuck felt there was something missing in his spiritual life. He decided it was time to look beyond the ashrams and the gurus for something else that would fulfill him. He decided to take a look at the life of Jesus.

Tuck went to the local Catholic church and joined the RCIA group to find answers to many of his questions. He finally found what he'd been seeking for so many years.

"The more I learned from what Jesus said and from what the Catholic Church teaches, the more I realized that *that* was the source of ultimate truth. I even got to the point where I said that Hindus know how to ask all the right questions and Jesus knows all the right answers." Tuck looks at his journey in this way: "It was all a search for God and a theory, whereas when Jesus came into the world, there was no need for theory any more. You had the actual 'God among us.' And that experience is something no other religion can offer."

He looks back with a new perspective at the books he used to read from the ashram.

"I pick up those books and I look at them," says Tuck. "And it does very much seem to me that they are a series of theories and questions rather than a series of answers. The answers come from books like the Bible and St. Teresa of Avila, St. Catherine, St. Thérèse of Lisieux, and Mother Teresa. Those are answers that are grounded in the truth. I'm sure that I went through all that searching in order that I might appreciate the full benefit of becoming a Catholic."

Tuck has stayed active in the RCIA and is now sponsoring a young man named John who will be joining the Church this Easter. But making the decision to become a sponsor wasn't easy for Tuck.

"I've been avoiding it because I didn't think I was really qualified to do it," he says. The man who was originally supposed to be John's sponsor prayed about it, and God told him to let Tuck do it. "I said, 'OK, if that's what's supposed to happen.' And John and I have been working together now. And we're getting to be quite good friends."

As much as Tuck enjoys the classes and people he works with in the RCIA, there's an even bigger reason he continues to devote so much time to the Church. Tuck says, "The most gratifying part of being in the Christian religion is the friendship that I've developed with Jesus and His father and our Blessed Mother. I've become more and more aware of everything that's been done for me and for everyone in this wonderful world that we have here."

Being a part of the RCIA has allowed Tuck to feel the presence of God working in his life in a deep way. He says, "The RCIA is the most important thing you can do in the Church. There's nothing more important than bringing people into the Church. People are outside the Church, you bring them through the door, they look around, and then they make up their mind. But they can't make up their mind if they don't come through the door. So I think that bringing people through the door of the Church and presenting them to the Holy Spirit, so to speak, is the most important thing, the most wonderful thing you can do in your life. That's why I like the RCIA best of all the ministries that I'm involved with."

If we believe what Tuck says is true, then it's time we all checked out the RCIA programs in our own parishes. We might be surprised at what a difference it can make in our spiritual lives.

Tucker Coon remains active in his parish, still attending all meetings of the RCIA in various capacities, leading groups in lectio divina, the rosary, and centering prayer in Christian meditation. He leads the Chaplet of Divine Mercy every morning before Mass. "So I still have my hours of morning prayers as I did before," he says, "and best of all, it's in the Catholic Church, where all my questions have answers." | Aired: April 2, 2007

***
MOVED TO ACTION: QUESTIONS FOR THOUGHT

1. Jennifer Fulwiler was adamant in asking tough questions about the Catholic faith and in getting answers. Have you ever had a question about your faith that you wanted an answer to but haven't taken the time to ask? Have you received an answer that makes you uneasy? Have you truly explored all avenues—books, the *Catechism,* your pastor—in getting your answer?

2. Joseph Pearce was brought to the Catholic Church in part by reading classic Catholic authors. What books, movies, or other media have you been exposed to lately that bring you closer to your faith? Is there a person in your life who has been a big influence in bringing you closer to God? Have you thanked him or her?

3. We tend to believe that miracles, like Saul's conversion, rarely occur. But Kari Beckman recognized having three miracles in her life. Do you think that there may possibly have been miracles in your own life but you just didn't recognize them? Think about it.

4. We live today in a very secularized world. Steven Mosher was a part of that world when he finally realized that God had a better plan for all of us on this planet. Are you sometimes swayed by popular belief instead of holding to your faith? Are you able to articulate your belief to others? If not, what can you do to change that?

5. Tuck Coon can't seem to say enough about the RCIA program in his parish. Have you ever been involved in yours? Have you ever thought about being a sponsor? What do you think you might learn?

CHAPTER | FOUR |

FROM SHEPHERD BOY TO KING DAVID
Drastic Job Changes

Samuel said to Jesse, "Are all your sons here?" And he said, "There remains yet the youngest, but he is keeping the sheep." And Samuel said to Jesse, "Send and bring him, for we will not sit down until he comes here." He sent and brought him in. Now he was ruddy, and had beautiful eyes, and was handsome. The Lord said, "Rise and anoint him; for this is the one."

—1 Samuel 16:11–12

I'm All Shook Up

It's not every day you hear about a successful advertising executive giving it all up to become a religious sister. And if you had known Sr. Mary Ann Foggin, s.g.l. when she was just Mary Ann Foggin, you'd be surprised as well.

"Like most young people, when I got out of college I had as my goal to be a success," says Sr. Mary Ann. "I wasn't very faith-driven; in fact,

I wasn't faith-driven at all. All I really cared about was finding a career that would allow me to make a lot of money and live a life of luxury. That was my goal."

Mary Ann eventually found a job she loved in advertising and worked for two different agencies over a period of fourteen years.

"I was fortunate in that I was able to make some good money and I fulfilled a lot of my dreams," she says. "I traveled around Europe. I had nice clothes, and I pampered myself with manicures and hundred-dollar haircuts. And that, to me, was success. For a long time that was my vision, and I was very content. When I hit thirty, I thought, OK, I've accomplished pretty much what I wanted. I had a house and a serious boyfriend. That was the point at which I thought, OK, now I can enter into phase two of my life. Little did I know that the Lord's version of phase two of my life was very different from what I thought phase two was going to be."

The advertising company Mary Ann worked for was downsizing, and she became aware that the job security she had enjoyed might be coming to an end. At the same time, the man she was involved with left the country for a new job and put their relationship permanently on hold.

"The Lord shook things up," says Sr. Mary Ann, "and I wasn't prepared for that. I wasn't grounded in the Lord. I was brought up Catholic, but I didn't have faith. I had no relationship with the Lord. And I didn't know how to fix all these things that were sort of falling apart in my life."

At that point, Mary Ann picked up a book her mother had given to her.

"It was *The Message of Medjugorje*. I read it in just a few hours one night. It spoke about Mary's appearing and asking us to convert, to turn our lives around, to put Jesus first. I have had a connection with the

Blessed Mother my entire life. And I'm sure it's because of my name and my mom's devotion to Mary. For me, she was my connection to heaven. I had never heard that Mary was appearing in modern times. So I just couldn't believe it. I couldn't put the book down."

While the apparitions in Medjugorje, Bosnia and Herzegovina, have not been officially approved by the Catholic Church, they have been a source of inspiration to many. When Mary Ann fell asleep that night, a sense of peace came upon her that she hadn't felt in a long time.

"In a dream, I saw a figure in the distance, walking back and forth," says Sr. Mary Ann. "I thought the person must be looking for something. I asked, 'Oh, are you looking for something?' The person looked at me and he said, 'No, I've found you.' And I don't know why, but the first thing that came to my mind was *Oh, this is Jesus.*

"I didn't take my eyes off him. Then he went dazzlingly white, brilliant white. I was so transfixed by this that I couldn't move. Eventually he disappeared, and I woke up at that moment. I'm a very rational person, but I knew it was the Lord. I just lay in that bed, thinking, *Oh my gosh. He found me. He really found me.* And that was the turning point for me."

Mary Ann hadn't been to Sunday Mass in years, let alone a weekday Mass, but that next morning she felt compelled to go.

"At the consecration, I just started to sob," she recalls. "For the first time in my life, I really knew and believed with my heart, my mind, my body, and my soul that that was Jesus Christ. I was rediscovering my faith all over again in a way I had never, ever related to as a child. And it was powerful for me."

Mary Ann became a daily communicant and began her reconversion to the Catholic faith. It took another few years, after much prayer and discernment, before she decided to quit her job and move on to something else without the comfort of having another job to go to.

"The bonus check I got was exactly, to the penny, the money that covered my living expenses until the day I joined the Servants of God's Love," says Sr. Mary Ann. She joined the order nine years ago, at the age of forty. She is now very busy using her business and public-relations skills working with young people, helping them to discern if they might have a calling. She is the vocations director for the Diocese of Lansing.

"The Lord gave me the courage to just go ahead and do what he was asking, because I cannot imagine my life any other way," she says.

Not everyone hears the voice of God as clearly as Sr. Mary Ann did in her dream. Many of us struggle to recognize God's will in our lives. Sr. Mary Ann shares a key ingredient to becoming a better listener: "Most of us—and I was the same before my reconversion—are very uncomfortable with silence. But you must have some quiet in your life in order to be attuned to what the Holy Spirit is doing and to be able to recognize God's voice when He speaks to you.

"Get comfortable with silence and start to pray, because it can change your life."

Since August 2011, Sr. Mary Ann Foggin, S.G.L., has been working in campus ministry at St. Catherine of Siena Academy in Wixom, Michigan. She also works at a house of discernment for women off campus of the University of Michigan. In six years they have had six women from the house join religious life, and two more are heading in that direction in 2012. Sr. Mary Ann says, "It is a privilege to spend my days with young women who are eager to take their identity and dignity from being rooted in Christ. The Lord is at work and I am so grateful to be at His service." | Aired: October 1, 2007

✷ ✷ ✷
Living Life Six Feet Under

Dale Robinson, from St. Louis, has had an interesting string of jobs. At the age of thirteen, he started work at a funeral home. From there he went to work in the coroner's office, and for many years after that he was a homicide detective, investigating upward of ninety-five homicides a year. Dale recognizes the value of what he's learned from having dealt with death for such a long time, and he is eager to pass his wisdom on to others.

"It's a different type of job," Dale says. "You know the worst thing that ever happens to anybody happened to them before I got a phone call. My job began when their life ended."

Notifying a family that they have lost a loved one was never easy for Dale, but his faith kept him going.

"You have to believe that God loves you," he says. "And God's going to be standing right beside you. Because if God wasn't standing there holding your hand, no human being I know of could walk in and tell a family that their life has just been exploded apart. You have to have God holding your hand."

"When it comes to death, you know, when it first hits you, you don't think about the heavenly reward, being with Christ for eternity. All you feel is your heart breaking. There was a period of time when I lost seven family members in four years, and one of them was my daughter. It was a very difficult time for me. And it took me a while to get back onto the straight path and realize what God wanted."

Looking back now, Dale knows that God was preparing him for the ministries he would be a part of later on in his life.

"When I retired I told my wife, 'I know God wants me to do more than I'm doing, but I don't know what it is.' She told me to pray on it. So

I prayed and I prayed and I prayed. I realized that what I've dealt with all my life is death. And having seen what people go through, I thought that this might be a place for me to be of help. Turns out it was. I love bereavement ministry because of the help you can give someone."

Dale learned how to care for the bereaved through his own personal experiences as well as by praying with and spending time with all those families who had lost loved ones throughout his years with the homicide squad. He continues to use his gift of compassion in the bereavement ministry. Dale says, "I think it all boils down to the fact that Christ loves you. And all He wants you to do is be kind to one another in every circumstance in life; whether it be in death, feeding the hungry, visiting those in prisons, or whatever. Death is not the end, it's just the beginning."

Dale spreads his unique joyful attitude in many other ministries at his home parish of Our Lady Queen of Peace, including a prison ministry at a federal jail. He is awed by the reverence he sees in the inmates when they go to chapel.

"The important thing is to see them and help them and talk about Christ," Dale says. "I wish I could take every parish and set them inside that chapel—it's impossible to do because of security—and set them inside this nondenominational chapel, so they could see these men enter in a line to accept the body of Christ. Tears come from their eyes after receiving Communion. We have no kneelers, since it's nondenominational, but they'll kneel by their chair or kneel down and put their head on their chair for twenty or thirty minutes and weep. When we talk about entering into the mystery of Christ at the Eucharist, I think we could learn a lot from everyone if we just took the time."

"Of all the things I do in the Church, from prison ministry to disability ministry to serving as eucharistic minister, the best assignment I have is being a greeter, because you get to say hello to someone and mean it, to smile at them and open the door for them out from the gathering area and say, 'Guess who's inside waiting for you?'

"I love people. When it comes to the Sign of Peace I cross the aisle, I bow like I'm supposed to, and I cross the aisle and work the crowd on the other side. I just love people. I think Christ wants you to be happy. And I think Christ wants you to enjoy one another.

"As long as God wants me here, I know it's part of my plan. So I hobble along, sing a song, and try to make people as happy as I possibly can and do what I think He wants me to do."

Dale Robinson passed away on June 23, 2010, from surgery complications. Dale's widow, Roseann, says, "I would be very proud to have Dale's interview turned into a story line for the book. He lived his faith daily right up to the end." He will be missed. | Aired: February 16, 2006

***

THE AMERICAN DREAM…IN HAITI?

Forty-three-year-old Patrick Moynihan is a deacon, husband, father, and modern-day missionary. Missionary work is not what you would have expected of him if you had looked at his life back in 1995. He was living the American dream, by most people's standards. He worked as a futures and options trader at Louis Dreyfus Corporation in Connecticut, and he was very good at what he did. Yet Patrick was looking for more.

"We were already a practicing Catholic family, going to church and very much in love with our faith, but we went through a deepening metanoia, a deepening conversion," Patrick explains. "In particular, the challenge came in Matthew 6:25 and on, where Jesus talks about the birds of the field, and how they don't toil but God takes care of them, and how much more important we are than birds. Why worry about these things? Do what God asks you to do. And that just finally, as we say, broke the bank—that and the community in the Acts of the Apostles. The description of the early Christian community is very important."

Patrick's brother Brian was involved with a school starting up in Haiti that allowed some of the poorest children in that country to gain an education. Patrick saw a need that he felt he could fill, thanks in part to what he had learned in the business world.

"I really enjoyed working for Louis Dreyfus," he says. "And as St. Thomas Aquinas says, 'Grace builds on nature.' A tremendous amount that I had learned as a trader was extremely important to me as a missionary in a country as wild and crazy as Haiti, in terms of currency devaluation, change in the prices, and how economics works. I had been given these talents and I had been using them to my own reward, and I decided I could just rely on God and use them to other people's reward."

Patrick moved his family to Haiti and became the head of the school and president of The Haitian Project. He felt strongly that since he'd been given a good education that was paid for by his parents, he should do likewise and help others receive an education.

"The right thing to do was to give back what I'd been given so freely," Patrick says. "And that, of course, is scriptural too—Matthew 10:8. And that is a huge part of our missionary work. What you receive for free, you must give for free. The Scripture was extremely important in our decision to become a missionary family."

The Haitian Project operates a private Catholic secondary boarding school that serves more than three hundred academically gifted children from economically disadvantaged families.

"It was a school with the right mission," says Patrick. "The idea is to educate kids from the poorest neighborhoods who are academically gifted and to give them the opportunity to get back into the education system and go on to university.

"The school now is based solidly around three pieces of Scripture. Thessalonians says, 'If you do not work, you cannot eat': self-reliance. The school is very much about building one's personal self-reliance to the benefit of others. The second piece of Scripture that's extremely important at the school is 'What you receive free, you must give for free.' And the last would be putting others first; it's the general gospel message of Jesus Christ."

Deacon Patrick and his family moved back to the States, to South Carolina. He became president emeritus of The Haitian Project. He was looking forward to what God had in store next for him and his family.

"I think purpose keeps me motivated," he says. "Having experienced so much being involved with God's purpose and God's miracle, you just want to get back at it. With God, it's like walking up to the plate and hitting a home run, time and time again. If you just dedicate yourself to His work you get to be involved in such amazing miracles. I like to be part of the challenge that we all have from the gospels: to convert. As John the Baptist says, 'To make straight the path.' There's always an opportunity to straighten out the crooked path."

Deacon Patrick Moynihan and his family are back in Haiti. Deacon Moynihan serves as president of The Haitian Project (THP) and its tuition-free Catholic boarding school, a post he held from 1996 to 2006 and returned to in March 2009. In addition to his work with THP, Deacon Moynihan is a deacon for the Rockford diocese. With his wife, Christina, along with their four children, he has decided to stay in Haiti "ad infinitum." To learn more about The Haitian Project, go to www.haitianproject.org. | Aired: September 29, 2008

***

You Can Call Me Mister, Doctor, Father

At seventy-one, an age when most priests are nearing retirement, Fr. Don Forsythe is just getting started. The widower, father of ten, grandfather, and former chief of anesthesiology at Holy Spirit Hospital in Pennsylvania decided, in his mid-sixties, to become a priest.

Born Patrick Don Bosco Forsythe, in Ireland, Fr. Don, as he is now known, considered a vocation to the priesthood when he was an altar boy, but eventually he decided to pursue a career in medicine. He married and moved to the United States, where he became a citizen and, along with his wife, Ann, raised ten children, one of whom died at two months.

In 1996, Ann became ill with an untreatable form of leukemia. It was during this time that Don's thoughts of the priesthood returned. He was sixty-three years old.

"The thought came back into my head," Fr. Don explains, "but I dismissed it. I was two years away from retirement. Then, about six months before Ann died, she came into the bedroom where I was reading and she just said, 'Don, you should be a priest.' It startled me, but I didn't let on that she had read my mind. I dismissed the subject again, and six months later, Ann died.

"Six months after Ann's death, I was invited to dinner at the home of some friends who are Lutheran. We were laughing and joking during dinner, and my friend Joe turned to me and said, 'Don, have you ever thought about being a priest?' I said, 'Joe, where did that come from? I'm too old.' But for some reason that sort of tweaked me, and I decided to do something about it. I prayed to the Holy Spirit for discernment. I didn't pray to be a priest and I didn't pray not to be a priest. I just wanted to have the right answer, whether that be yes or no."

Fr. Don tried five times to be considered for the priesthood; each time he was turned down because of his age. Then a priest friend directed him to the Diocese of Birmingham, where an exception was made, and he was allowed to enter the seminary and begin studying for the priesthood. At first, Don found himself overwhelmed by the workload.

"I was carrying seventeen credits the first semester, and it was going in one [ear] and out the other," he recalls. "I thought I'd made a big mistake. But after about two months, I got mad, and I went to the chapel and I said, 'Look, Lord, you called me, I didn't call you. Now give me the tools and let me do this job.' Two weeks later everything started clicking."

Before he finished at the seminary, Fr. Don had quadruple-bypass heart surgery. Though most people would have considered such a major operation a big setback, Fr. Don says his time in the hospital allowed him to focus on his studies and prepare for his final exams.

He was ordained a priest on June 5, 2004, in Birmingham. After serving only two months with a monsignor and another priest at a large parish in Birmingham, Fr. Don was approached by the bishop, who asked him to go to Tuscumbia, Alabama, to run Our Lady of the Shoals parish, by himself, for an ailing pastor.

"It's been great," Fr. Don reports. "The people here have been very welcoming. The thing I love best is confession. I find that my life experience—my knowledge of medicine, and my having raised a family—is great background for advising penitents. I've had so many blessings in this life that I have to pay back the Lord."

Fr. Don Forsythe is now seventy-eight years old. He was stationed at a parish in Talladega for a year but was brought back to pastor Our Lady of the Shoals Church in Tuscumbia after the previous pastor retired. He still works there, even though he lost his leg last year and uses a prosthesis to walk. He says, "I guess I'll keep working until they put me in a box." | Aired: February 21, 2005

The Thrill of Victory

Twenty-seven might seem like a very young age at which to retire. But for Chase Hilgenbrinck, it was the exact right time. Chase was at the top of his game, playing professional soccer for the New England Revolution, when he decided to follow his heart and shocked soccer fans across the country by joining the seminary.

"At that time I just felt blessed that I was able to play on such a good team, to finish my career on such a high note," says Chase.

Chase had played soccer in college, at Clemson. After graduating with a bachelor's degree in Spanish and international trade, he went to Chile as a professional soccer player. Signing first with CD Huachipato of the Chilean first division, he subsequently played for Deportes Naval, and then went on to win the second-division title in 2006 with the league sensation, Ñublense. Chase played the 2007 season with Ñublense in the first division, completing his fourth and final year in the Chilean league.

"I certainly had very special experiences playing soccer in South America," says Chase. "The passion that they have for the game is not even comparable to the NFL or Major League Baseball here. It's much more passionate. These people *live* for the game of soccer. They *live* for their teams."

After returning to the United States, Chase played briefly for the Colorado Rapids before joining the New England Revolution.

At the time Chase decided to retire, the New England Revolution happened to be ranked number one in Major League Soccer (MLS). Retiring when your team is winning would seem to be a difficult thing to do. But Chase was comfortable with his decision.

"When I went to the Revolution, I already knew that I was going to be a seminarian in August, so I had time to prepare for it," says Chase.

"Really, my time with the Revolution, and all my time back here in the States while I was playing in the MLS, was just an opportunity for me to enjoy the game with no pressure on my shoulders. Knowing that my future was not in soccer, that I wasn't playing for money or playing for contracts, was freeing. I was just playing for the innocence of the game and for the love of the game."

Chase's decision to enter the seminary wasn't made overnight. He knows there were some pivotal moments for him. "It's strange to look back and see how the Lord has called me all of my life without my really noticing or seeing it," he says. "I actually felt like this was something serious in my life when I was in Chile. It was a time when I had left my family and friends behind in the States."

"I realized that the Lord's plan for me was to be alone to be able to hear His voice in my life, to hear His will for my life. I started to develop my personal relationship with Christ because I was alone. I needed somebody. I needed comfort, and I fell back on what I knew. My parents were the ones who instilled the faith in me from a very young age. And during that deep personal prayer was when I first heard the call to the priesthood, although it wasn't something that I wanted to hear. It certainly wasn't the thing that I wanted for myself at that time, especially not when I was a professional athlete and living out my dream." But Chase continued to pay attention to the call.

"As I thought about my success in soccer, about having accomplished a lot of the things I had dreamed of doing, I realized that it wasn't enough for me, that it wasn't going to sustain me for the rest of my life," Chase says. "And this call to the priesthood really had something to it. There was something behind it."

Chase sometimes wondered if he could have made a bigger impact by continuing to play professional soccer and witnessing in that way instead of becoming a priest. But he received the answer to that question loud and clear.

"I thought I was going to become a huge soccer star, famous, make a lot of money, like every kid's dream. And I achieved a lot of great things," says Chase. "But it wasn't until I told everybody that I was going to be a priest, that I wanted to be a seminarian, that I started giving interviews—daily. I appeared on ESPN, in *USA Today*, and just about every newspaper in the country. I was on Fox News and all of these other great media outlets."

Chase realized that all that publicity was a strong confirmation of the path he was supposed to be on. "I was already making more of an impact as a seminarian than I ever did as an athlete," he says. "I could never live the life I wanted to live and be totally giving of myself to my faith if soccer was my priority. And that's when I understood that this was what my soul was truly searching for."

Chase is now studying at Mount St. Mary's Seminary in Maryland and is on track to become a diocesan priest for the Peoria diocese in Illinois. He's looking forward to many new changes and challenges.

"It is a little bit daunting, the task that lies ahead," Chase says, "but at the same time it's not going to deter me from doing God's will. I feel like I'm up for the challenge. Of course soccer has prepared me to be competitive, to be disciplined, to persevere, to be a leader, and to do many things that will help me out in the priesthood."

"You basically live life with others," Chase explains. "You're there for their most happy and sad times in life. A priest is a man who has to love people as Christ did. I have to be that witness. And that's something I look forward to doing—just being that witness to people. I want to be a good priest for the Church. And I want to be that example of the Lord."

Chase Hilgenbrinck is a former professional soccer defender and current seminarian of the Diocese of Peoria, studying at Mount St. Mary's Seminary in Emmitsburg, Maryland. | Aired: August 3, 2009

***
Moved to Action: Questions for Thought

1. Sr. Mary Ann Foggin had a vivid dream in which she felt she encountered Jesus. Have you ever felt the presence of God in a very real way through a dream, a person, or an event? What did you do about it?
2. Dale Robinson felt that God had a plan for his life, and he prayed about it. How often have you prayed for guidance in your life? How well did you listen?
3. Deacon Patrick Moynihan gave up a lucrative career to follow God's will in his life. Have you ever been asked to give up something that was too hard to give up? What did you learn from Patrick's experience?
4. Fr. Don Forsythe decided late in life to change drastically the path he was on. Most people thought he was too old to become a priest. Are there times in your life when you feel that someone or something is trying to stop you from doing what the Lord is calling you to do?
5. Chase Hilgenbrinck left a promising career in soccer to become a priest. How do you think society views this choice? Have you ever felt called to make a drastic change that you weren't sure was God's will for your life? How did you respond?

CHAPTER | FIVE |

THE WISDOM OF SOLOMON
Thinking Outside the Box

So the king said, "Bring me a sword," and they brought a sword before the king. The king said, "Divide the living boy in two; then give half to one, and half to the other." But the woman whose son was alive said to the king—because compassion for her son burned within her—"Please, my lord, give her the living boy; certainly don't kill him!" The other said, "It shall be neither mine nor yours; divide it." Then the king responded: "Give the first woman the living boy; do not kill him. She is his mother."
—1 Kings 3:24–27

THE ALMIGHTY DOLLAR

One Sunday at St. Bartholomew Catholic Faith Community in Wayzata, Minnesota, one hundred parishioners walked out of church each a hundred dollars richer than when they walked in. It was the beginning of the Kingdom Assignment, which is based on the parable in the Gospel of Matthew about a man who gives each of his three servants a sum of money and we learn what use each makes of it.

Jill Kohler had read a book about another congregation that had done a project based on this gospel passage. She shared the idea with the social-justice committee at St. Bartholomew. Here, she explains what happened the day their pastor, Fr. Michael Reding, proclaimed that parable to the congregation and then put it into action.

"He said he wanted us to take a Kingdom Assignment," Jill says. "And he said he needed volunteers. He didn't give any description of the project; he just said, 'I need volunteers.'

"Of course, there was dead silence at the beginning, when he called for volunteers. People just kind of looked up at him and at each other. And then one by one you started to see some hands go up, and Father would say, 'Come on up, come on up.' The next thing he did, he turned to them and took out of his pocket a wad of hundred-dollar bills and began handing them out to each of the volunteers. At that point, the whole congregation was gasping, everyone wishing they had volunteered. Then Father explained that the money he was handing out was not his, and it was not the church's, but that it was God's money." Just as in the gospel story, the plan was for each of the volunteers to put the money to good use.

"The idea was, take this, grow it, do something with it that you believe should be done in the world," says Jill. "Father wanted them to use the money to do God's work. And he said that by taking the money, they were agreeing that in three months' time they would come back and tell us how they had spent it. Fr. Michael made it clear that the money he was giving out was coming from a donation that had been given to the social justice committee and was not coming out of the budget from some other ministry in the parish."

Most of the volunteers felt an obligation to do something worthwhile with their hundred dollars. Jill recounts what one businessman had to say.

"He said, 'I deal with millions of dollars every day, and I can't tell you how much heavier this hundred dollars is than what I deal with on a daily basis.' One of the points Fr. Michael wanted to make was that all of the money we have is God's money."

Parishioners of all different ages volunteered for the project. There were traditional ways of using the money, such as food drives, as well as some unusual and creative uses.

"A father and teenage daughter volunteered together," says Jill. "They decided to adopt a dog through Helping Paws and train it. They train dogs for disabled people, and it's a two-year commitment. Another person took his hundred dollars and went to his grandkids and said, 'I'm going to multiply these hundred dollars. I'm going to give you each one hundred dollars, and I want you to talk with me about what you're going to do with it.' I thought that was a great way to teach kids."

One woman put her money into training so she could become a court volunteer for children. Another had a wine-tasting party and raised almost eight hundred dollars for a battered-women's shelter. Another parishioner challenged her six-year-old son to take ten dollars and grow it. He hosted a party with some friends and collected seventy-one dollars, which he gave to his teacher's five-year-old grandson, whose mother had died.

"We had some wonderful stories as a result of this project," Jill says. "And I am sure anybody who does this would have some wonderful stories, because I think people are looking for ways to do good, and in most cases they just need a little push."

Jill Kohler is a parishioner and volunteer at St. Bartholomew Catholic Faith Community in Wayzata, Minnesota. | Aired: April 18, 2005

***

Mary's Special Touch

Sixty-two-year-old Cheri Lomonte has had a special bond with Mary, the Mother of God, since she was little. When she was ten, Cheri knew something was wrong with her own mother. At the time, the doctors and Cheri didn't understand that her mother was suffering from mental illness. So Cheri looked elsewhere for the comfort she wasn't able to receive from her own mother.

"That sent me to Mary, our Mother," Cheri says. "I remember kneeling in front of Mary at church and asking her if she would be my mother."

Mary continued to be present as Cheri married and raised her six children. But later in life, Mary grew even more prominent in Cheri's life. Cheri took up photography, with a specialty in taking pictures of Marian statues. She became well known for her Madonnas. About ten years ago she was asked to take a picture of the oldest Madonna in the United States—La Conquistadora in Santa Fe, New Mexico.

"I used to learn as much as I could about what I was going to photograph," Cheri says. "I went into the first bookstore [I saw] and I said, 'Do you have anything on La Conquistadora, on Mother Mary?' The clerk looked up at me and said, 'No, we don't have anything on Mary, but why don't you write a book about her?'"

Cheri thought the interaction was strange, but she also knew it was important.

"You must remember," she says, "that I am the person who says every morning, 'Here I am Lord, your servant, what can I do for you today? May my eyes and my ears and my heart be open so I can hear Your message.' But the problem was, oops, I'm not a writer. This was going to be interesting. I'm not a Mariologist. I love Mary, but I'm no expert on her."

Then Cheri began to recall all the stories she'd heard from the people who would help her get the Madonnas ready for her photo sessions. They would tell her stories about how Mary had affected their lives.

"I got it," she said. "I thought, OK, I'm supposed to tell these stories. And with every story I heard, my faith grew."

Cheri collected the stories and published them in a book, *The Healing Touch of Mary*. She sold around thirteen thousand copies, a respectable number, given that she published the book herself. But that wasn't enough for Cheri.

"I kept hearing that more people need to hear these stories," she says. "It has to reach a bigger audience. I got the idea, and it was divinely inspired, to do a radio show. I wanted to do it to honor Mary, and for all the beautiful things she's given me in my life. And I do believe Mary was asking me to do this. This was my calling."

Cheri created *Mary's Touch*, a weekly half-hour radio program that shares the stories of people touched by Mary. She also brought along a Catholic theologian, Sally Robb, to cohost the show with her. *Mary's Touch* is beginning its third year of production. It won the prestigious Gabriel Award from the Catholic Academy for Communication Arts Professionals for the best radio program in the United States and Canada. And in just two short years it has a thriving website and is heard on a hundred stations in the United States and in fifty foreign countries.

"It usually takes much longer for that to happen," Cheri says. "You usually have to be in the business for five to ten years. That should tell you that this is a divinely inspired program; when we start recording, we say our prayers and then we let the Holy Spirit do the rest."

Cheri has written two more books of stories. With the proceeds from her books and online donations, she's able to keep producing her inspiring program.

"We get e-mails like you would not believe," says Cheri. "We get stories from people who listen to the show, and they say, 'This is what it's done for me.' I don't know where Mother Mary is taking this but I'm along for the best ride of my life."

Cheri Lomonte is executive director and founder of Mary's Touch *radio broadcast and the Frontline Faith Project. The mission of the program is to remind us all of the grace and unconditional love that Mother Mary brings to the world. The Frontline Faith Project distributes compact MP3 players, preloaded with Catholic content, to members of our armed forces currently deployed. Find Cheri's projects at www.marystouch.org and www.frontlinefaithproject.org. | Aired: December 6, 2009*

***

EXTREME MAKEOVER CATHOLIC-STYLE

Extreme Makeover: Home Edition has nothing on Holy Name of Jesus parishioners in Medina, Minnesota. Working together, in four and a half months, they put a one-thousand-square-foot addition on the home of Georgia and Jeff Novak, for the Novaks' twenty-four-year-old quadriplegic daughter, Angie. And they didn't even resort to large corporate sponsors to get it done.

Fr. Jonathan Licari, pastor of Holy Name of Jesus parish, tells how it all got started: "Angie's three young cousins wrote me a letter, and I called the young women's mother, Angie's aunt. She described how her daughters looked on Angie as their hero because she's been able to make it through some very difficult situations in her life, especially being a quadriplegic, and yet somehow was able to keep her sense of humor and her sense of direction and purpose in life. What they were asking of the parish, through me, was 'Can you help?' Angie had a limited living area in her parents' home. I don't think it was much more than ten or fifteen feet of space to move around in. From her bedroom to the kitchen, and that was it."

Angie has been dependent on a ventilator since she was hit by a car in 1994 while crossing the street on her bicycle. After talking to Angie's aunt, Fr. Jonathan called Dan Gallagher, an architect in the parish, and asked if he and his wife would look at the place and see if something could be done.

"Before they even left, they already promised that they would do something," says Fr. Jonathan. "And it was just a snowball effect after that. People continued to get on board with the program. We started lining up all of the things that would need to be done to put an addition on someone's home."

Eventually, more than six hundred parishioners stepped up to volunteer and help make this dream a reality. Most of them spent every weekend working at Angie's place, and some were there every day.

"We put a complete handicap-accessible addition onto her parents' home," Fr. Jonathan says. "It's all climate-controlled. We put in a generator in case there's a power failure. She has limited time with battery backup on her respirator. It's like we built Angie a house onto her parents' home—and we paid for it. It took the effort of everyone who contributed either money or time or service or skill to make it happen. It would not have been possible otherwise, because we could not have afforded to buy that kind of help. We could never have hired out the construction and got it done as quickly or as well, because the people who stepped forward here are all at the top of their game with their abilities."

Angie was very grateful to all the people who helped make this possible. Now she has her own space—something she thought would never happen.

"Mostly Angie has been overwhelmed by this whole thing," says Fr. Jonathan. "It will take her a while to really realize that it's hers. She has space to move around in. And it provided an opportunity for people to get to know each other, to see that generosity of spirit and charity coming from people, and to enjoy themselves doing it through some of the hottest weather of this season."

Angie's cousins saw an awesome person, someone who graduated from high school with honors, who paints beautiful pictures (she holds the paintbrush in her mouth), who has published poetry, and who takes classes over the Internet. Angie may be confined to her wheelchair and limited by her respirator, but that hasn't stopped her from living a complete and fulfilling life and touching others in a special way.

"Some of it is just so straightforward and gospel-oriented," says Fr. Jonathan. "Let's not stand around debating the concept or the issue, we have work to do. It started with a letter from three young women and it grew into a house. That's what happened."

Fr. Jonathan Licari, o.s.b., has taught theology and canon law at St. John's University. No longer pastor at Holy Name of Jesus, he is on the board of regents for St. John's University and is currently the subprior of St. John's Abbey in Collegeville, Minnesota. | Aired: January 9, 2006

***

What's a Nice Jew Doing at the Vatican?

In 1987, Gilbert Levine, a world-renowned conductor from Brooklyn, was invited to take a permanent position as conductor for the Krakow Philharmonic in Poland. It was the first such post for any American in the Eastern Bloc. It was this "new" historic first, an American living and working in the communist hometown of Pope John Paul II, that came to the pope's attention via Cardinal Macharski. A nice Jewish boy from New York was about to become the maestro to one of the most beloved popes in recent history.

"I had never met a Catholic priest until I went to Poland," says Gilbert, "and the first Catholic priest I met was the cardinal archbishop of Krakow, Cardinal Macharski, who was the successor of John Paul II. The second Catholic priest I met was the private secretary to His Holiness in the Vatican, and the third priest was the pope himself."

Pope John Paul II had heard that Gilbert had conducted the symphony in his hometown of Krakow, and he invited him to the Vatican when he returned.

"He brought me into his private library for a tête-a-tête, which is a kind of papal audience. It was just the two of us. He wanted to meet me and get to know me, and he drew me into a kind of immediate closeness. Something emboldened me, and I said to him, 'I believe that you were put on this earth by God to make things right between our two people.' I said that to the pope, and he didn't say anything. He was shocked or deep in thought. He didn't say anything."

Pope John Paul asked that Gilbert conduct the concert for his tenth-anniversary celebration. It was the beginning of a seventeen-year friendship between them, which Gilbert recalls in his new book, *The Pope's Maestro*. Gilbert remembers having a private audience with the pope—Gilbert's wife and his mother-in-law, an Auschwitz survivor, were included—before his first papal concert.

"He went over and talked to my mother-in-law in Polish," Gilbert recalls. "She was a survivor, and he was a slave laborer, effectively, in the stone quarry during the war. And they had a language that was all their own. I could see on my mother-in-law's face that this was an incredibly deep and meaningful conversation for her. One of the incredible journeys that *The Pope's Maestro* tells about is the story of my mother-in-law's finding peace through her relationship with the Holy Father. She died in a small room—very, very modest—and on the wall were pictures of her mother and father, murdered by the Nazis, her brother who was murdered by the Nazis, and herself and the pope."

Gilbert went on to work with Pope John Paul on several concerts dealing with Jewish-Catholic relations, the most famous being the Papal Concert to Commemorate the Shoah (or Holocaust). After 9/11, he expanded his attention to include Islam.

"In 2004, we had a Papal Concert of Reconciliation," says Gilbert, "where he sat beside the chief rabbi of Rome and the chief imam of the mosque of Rome and basically heard music that was intended to bring peace to the world. I think he understood, came to understand through me, that music had that power of what I call 'at one-ment,' of bringing people together wordlessly. He called it 'a way of peace.' Not a *language* of peace, a *way* of peace. He had vision that no other man that I've ever met, no other person that I've ever met, had. And I was honored to be of use in the realization of that vision, to be heard, to have my ideas used in his vision of peace. So that I went to him with the idea for a concert for the Holocaust and he said, 'No, it should be a papal concert, I'll bring in the Vatican and I trust you. Let's do this for the world.' And it was broadcast all over the world."

In gratitude for Gilbert's service as maestro, John Paul II invested him as a knight commander of the Pontifical Equestrian Order of Saint Gregory the Great—the first pontifical knighthood awarded to an American Jew, and the first accorded to a nonecclesiastical musician since Mozart. He is now Sir Gilbert Levine.

"He honored my Jewish faith because for him faith was the most important thing—faith," Gilbert says. "He didn't try to convert me. He wanted us to come to peace with one another. I feel blessed, more than blessed; I feel a tremendous responsibility to fulfill that vision that John Paul had. I feel that very strongly, and it's what motivates my work."

Sir Gilbert Levine is honoring the desire of John Paul that he write his book, and he also continues to work on more musical pieces to help bring that shared vision of peace to the world.

"This book has a very strong message for everyone," says Sir Gilbert, "for Catholics, for Jews, for Muslims, for Protestants, for many, many people. Because this is about bringing us together to find peaceful solutions to what divides us, and that's hard to do. But I think we've found that way and *The Pope's Maestro* tells that story.

Sir Gilbert's life as "the pope's maestro" has been the subject of numerous television, radio, and newspaper stories and interviews, including a Polish television documentary and a 60 Minutes profile. Sir Gilbert was educated at Juilliard, Princeton, and Yale. He and his wife have two sons and live in New York. | Aired: December 27, 2010

***
Send in the Clowns

When someone mentions the word *clown*, what happens? Usually you get a lot of giggling and snickering. Sometimes people think back to their childhood, conjuring memories of being entertained by a colorful man or woman dressed up in ridiculous clothes. That giggling response is exactly what Gilbert and Charlotte Ardoin, both clowns, hope to elicit from their audiences.

What started out as just clowning around with their four children turned into a clown ministry for both of them, even though they were supposed to be retired.

Gilbert recalls how he and Charlotte first became interested in clowning: "I used to clown with the children. Charlotte and I were working in the CYO here in Baton Rouge for a long time, and we actually put clown costumes on one time for a school function. We used to do Santa Claus every year with the CYO and things like that."

Gilbert and Charlotte's daughter, Anne, who was interested in teaching through clowning, was working at a Vacation Bible School about five or six years ago and asked her parents for some help. "She said, 'Dad, I need some help with my clowning at my church, because it's hard to do just by myself. Please, can you help me?'" says Gilbert. "At first I told her I didn't think I wanted to. But she persisted, so we got to talking about it, and we prayed over it, and I agreed to help her."

Gilbert says, "It was fun. We came up with a few little skits here and there, and I told her, 'Look, if I'm going to be a clown, then I want to join Clown Alley [the local chapter of a national clowning association], and I want to find out more about it.' So we did. We joined Baton Rouge Clown Alley. There were about thirty-five clowns from all over the area, both secular clowns and some ministry clowns. After that we joined the

World Clown Association. Then we joined The Cross and the Clown. Most of our really good information has come from The Cross and the Clown clowning ministry."

Charlotte adds: "When Gilbert retired he said, 'Anywhere I go, you'll go with me.' And I thought to myself, Oh my! He wanted to do this clown work, and he kept asking me to do it. I felt I wasn't good at it, and I didn't want to do it. I always let him clown around with the kids but I never did it. But I went ahead to the clown school with him because I was interested enough to want to find out what goes on and what they do."

Charlotte started as the prop lady but soon moved on to clowning with the rest of them. Her stage name became "Miss Tag A. Long," since she had done that for a while before taking the leap into clowning. Gilbert is "Doktar Sproket" and their daughter Anne is "Joy." They became known as the Kingdom Clowns. And sometimes even Anne's daughter, Samantha, gets in on the act as "Sparkle."

The Ardoins have brought their clown ministry to Sunday schools, Vacation Bible Schools, day-care centers, school fairs, nursing homes, charity organizations, and hospitals. Gilbert says, "Wherever we go, we pray before we get there and we pray after we're done, thanking God, because He always goes ahead of us. He just clears everything out. It just makes it beautiful."

Charlotte remembers especially a visit they made to a hospital after Hurricane Katrina. "The very first day we walked into the hospital, it was like Jesus went before us," she says. "They told the children that clowns were coming, and they gave us a little wagon to use as we went around from room to room. People were coming up to us in the hallways, parents of children who were in intensive care, asking us to please come visit their children. We would go through and knock on the door and ask them if they would like to see a clown. If they said no, then we just gave them a gift and we didn't go in. If they said yes, then we'd bring the clown in. You could just see their little faces light up. It was the most awesome thing I think I have ever seen or done."

"It was just that the people knew we were Christians and they would come up and ask us to pray," says Gilbert. "And of course that was what it was all about."

Gilbert, Charlotte, and Anne often do skits that relate to Bible stories. They present these stories in humorous and entertaining ways and with a spirit of joy and enthusiasm, to keep the youngest and the oldest of their audience members riveted on the action.

Often, audience participation is required. One of their skits involves a flood, and as the water rises, the children get in on the act. "We wave higher and higher," Charlotte says. "And the children are waving too. They're all waving higher and higher. Then when the rains come, Anne runs out into the audience and squirts them with a little water. The children love it."

"It's fun," says Gilbert, smiling. "It's a show-and-tell thing. The whole thing about a clown ministry is that it's show and tell. That's what Jesus did. Ministry clowning is called 'the Jesus approach.'"

"We get the audience to participate, and while they're doing that, while they're having fun, they're learning," Charlotte says. "We're planting that seed of Jesus."

With the help of the outreach ministry of their parish in Baton Rouge, the Ardoins are able to purchase the small gifts that they leave with their audiences and to update their props as needed. For the Ardoins there's more to clowning around than just dressing up and trying to be funny. Bringing God's love and healing to others through humor is what they strive for, and they seem to be hitting the mark.

"The Lord is so good to us," says Gilbert. "He's been wonderful to our family. We're all pretty healthy, and it's just been a wonderful life for us. So we just go along with the Lord, wherever He leads us."

Seventy-five-year-old Gilbert Ardoin hasn't done any clowning at the hospitals since his wife Charlotte Ardoin passed away in 2010. But he says, "I'm still a clown at heart. I hope more people take up the ministry, because you can really have a great impact on people. And God can work through you in a joyful way." | Aired: August 7, 2006

***

MOVED TO ACTION: QUESTIONS FOR THOUGHT

1. St. Bartholomew's Catholic Faith Community came up with a unique way to encourage outreach in their parish. What do you think your parish could do to ignite that kind of fire in its parishioners? How could you help?
2. Cheri Lomonte came up with a way to demonstrate her love for Mary that ended up touching the hearts of many. She continued to listen to God's call even when she didn't think she could fulfill His will. Do you ever feel that you've been asked to do too much? What do you do? To whom do you turn?
3. Holy Name parishioners took it on themselves to do something for Angie. They didn't ask for outside help. They found a solution by calling on the congregation and their gifts. Do you know people whose gifts aren't being used to their potential? Are you using your God-given talents the way God would want?
4. Most popes wouldn't have chosen a Jewish musician to lead the music for a Catholic Mass. But it's that type of thinking that enabled Pope John Paul II to get the attention of the world and turn their eyes toward peace. How have you brought peace to the world where you live?
5. Gilbert and Charlotte Ardoin found a unique way to proclaim the Good News to others. Do you have a special talent that God could use to bring others closer to Him? Does someone you know have a special talent? Have you encouraged them to use it?

CHAPTER | SIX |

THE GOOD SAMARITAN
Who Is My Neighbor?

But a Samaritan while traveling came near him; and when he saw him, he was moved with pity. He went to him and bandaged his wounds, having poured oil and wine on them. Then he put him on his own animal, brought him to an inn, and took care of him.

—Luke 10:33–34

PLANTING ROOTS OF PEACE

When Britain's Princess Diana died suddenly in 1997, many people were sad for that country's loss of a regal humanitarian. What Heidi Kühn also thought about was the work Princess Diana had begun as an advocate for land-mine removal. Heidi, a mother of four and a member of St. Raphael parish in California, took it on herself to form Roots of Peace, one of many nongovernmental organizations working with the U.S. State Department to remove land mines.

"My background was as an international journalist," Heidi says. "I've seen a lot of things in my life, and I've never seen anything as cruel as land mines. Because of the international background, I was asked to host a group that was leading a nine-city tour on the issue of land mines. I thought of the vintners in northern California and the symbolism that grapes represent, and on two weeks' notice I gathered a hundred people in the living room of our home and I just made a toast from my heart that the world might go from mines to vines."

"It was literally an epiphany of sorts, the images of blood to wine, turning killing fields into bountiful vineyards. It is really Christ's lesson to us to turn blood into wine by turning swords into plowshares. We took that vision out of the living room of our home, and it's very proudly, strongly planted now in four countries—planting rice in Cambodia, grapes in Afghanistan, orchards in Croatia, and wheat in Iraq, with the vision that one day neighbor will be able to break bread with neighbor again."

Heidi has enlisted the help of many people, including her own family. Her daughter, Kyleigh, now seventeen and a senior in high school, went with her mother to Croatia when she was just thirteen to see firsthand how children were affected by this problem. Like her mother, Kyleigh was moved to take action.

Kyleigh recalls her impressions from that trip: "Seeing the plight of the children in Croatia at such an influential age really opened my eyes to the privilege that we have in America and the necessity that we have to share that privilege with other children across the world. I started a campaign called Making Change Work. It's a student-to-student program that seeks to empower children in a positive way to bring peace around the world. We distributed canisters to all the schools, and we had a youth ambassador at each school take up the torch at their own schools and asked for pennies. And it really works amazingly well. I couldn't believe we actually ended up raising seventy thousand dollars; that's seven million pennies."

"It's a fall campaign," Heidi explains. "It begins every September 11 and culminates on the last day of fall."

"As Catholics we have a duty to share our compassion with others in need," says Kyleigh. "When you get involved with the community, you're able to bring people together under one cause and take something that you feel strongly about and make a difference across the world."

"And I think through the Catholic Church, through our efforts, we can really engage people in a positive way," says Heidi. "I think that the power of hope, the power of love, the power of peace is so much stronger than the power of destruction. And field by field to take out land mines and to literally plant the roots of peace on earth is a small way in which we can win the war on terror, by removing the seeds of terror and literally planting peace on earth."

To date, Heidi and Kyleigh Kühn have raised more than fifty million pennies through the Roots of Peace Penny Campaign. Now, that's a mother-daughter team! Heidi has received many awards and recognitions on both a local and international level for her vision and work in creating a humanitarian organization. She has had the honor of attending four private audiences with Pope Benedict XVI at the Vatican. Roots of Peace is now embarking on a new program to remove land mines in the fields of Bethlehem and Qasr al-Yahud, the site of Jesus' baptism. There are an estimated 1.5 million land mines in the West Bank. Learn more at www.rootsofpeace.org. | Aired: December 29, 2004

***

DO IT FOR THE CHILDREN

Debbie Cornall's son Joe enlisted in the New York National Guard after 9/11. Shortly afterward, he was sent to Iraq for eleven months. While there, he found a way to involve his mother and his community.

Debbie recalls her conversation with Joe: "He said that in the little village where he was stationed there was a great need for children's clothes, for shoes, and for school supplies. And he said, 'Mom do you think there's something you can do to help?' I said, 'Absolutely. I'll try to do what I can.' I had no idea that it would turn out to be what it is.

"My younger son and I began by making posters. I called it the Child to Child project, and we asked for donated children's clothing, school supplies, and shoes. We put the posters up everywhere in Auburn; many, many people saw them, and after maybe a week or so people started bringing things here. I can't begin to tell you how much I had and still have, because I still continue to send the things over.

"In the beginning I was sending boxes, probably five or six a week. The people in my community were so generous. I can't tell you the number of times people came to my door and, sometimes never saying a thing, just handed me the things and started to cry and said that they were so glad to be able to help and would I please tell my son that they were thinking of him and praying for him."

Debbie's son is home now, but the soldiers who took his place are now accepting the boxes that Debbie and her community of Auburn, New York, continue to send. They send them to the community center in the Iraqi village, and from there they are distributed directly to the families who need the supplies.

"The captain of my son's unit sent me a DVD because I had sent so many boxes," Debbie says. "It showed them unloading the boxes and taking them to the community center, and the parents and the kids getting the things. It also showed some of the kids in school with some of the supplies that everyone had sent over. And, oh my gosh, it was something to see. Every time I look at it, I start to cry, because these kids have handfuls of things and they're sitting in school and it's just so exciting to know that we've all been a part of that."

Debbie isn't always sure that she'll find a way to get the boxes over, as it costs about twenty-five dollars to ship just one. She's shipped more than seventy-five boxes already.

"I pray all the time," says Debbie. "Sometimes I think I've sent my last box because I don't know where the money is going to come from for another one, and then somehow it comes, whether it's a random check in the mail from someone, or I'll say, 'God, if you want me to send another box, I don't know how I'm going to do it. You're going to have to guide me, something is going to have to happen, because I don't have any idea where I can get any more money.' And there's never been a time when it hasn't appeared. It was like everyone was waiting to help and they didn't know what to do and this gave them the opportunity to do what they would like to do.

"If I could do this for the rest of my life, I'd be happy, because it fills me with something, with so much love, and I can never say thank you enough to God for keeping my son alive. I had a very difficult time when he first went over. I got sick and had high blood pressure and I prayed a lot and I was better. I got through the rest of the time, and I could not have done that without God."

Debbie has a message for those people who aren't sure how to help: "If the opportunity comes about where you're able to help, try as hard as you can, because I don't think the military can do this alone. I think they do a wonderful job, but I think we need to help as well. We need to show the Iraqi people that we care about them and know what's going on over there and that we want to help them, too. I think it's our responsibility to do that for them."

Debbie Cornall's son Joe is serving another yearlong deployment in Afghanistan, which began November 2011. When Debbie learned that in the county where she lives there were no homeless shelters for women and children, she proceeded to set up a shelter for women and children in an apartment in her own home. A social service agency determines who may need Debbie's help. With the help of many volunteers, Debbie can accommodate up to six people in her home. She feels blessed to be an instrument of God in all she does. | Aired: August 8, 2005

My Faith Will Build It

Ninety-one-year-old Lucious Newsom has more energy and drive for his ministry than most of us would have at age twenty. In his long life, he has touched the lives of countless others. Lucious was a Baptist minister for thirty-five years in Chattanooga, Tennessee. After retiring, he was asked to speak in Indianapolis at a Thanksgiving dinner, which fed twenty thousand poor people. Lucious wanted to know what the servers and volunteers were doing for those people the day after Thanksgiving. When he learned that the volunteers could feed the poor only once a year, on Thanksgiving Day, Lucious felt his heart break. How were those people going to eat the rest of the year? Lucious didn't realize at the moment that this was the beginning of a new ministry for him.

Less than three weeks later, back home in Tennessee, he knew he had to listen to God's call to go back to Indianapolis and do something about the poverty he had seen.

"I left home," Lucious says. "I didn't have but one hundred dollars. And I didn't want anything. I believe that if God gives you a job, he'll take care of you. I came into Indianapolis. I looked to my right off the highway and there was a big ol' Kroger store, and they had some bread sitting out near the dumpster. I went in, and I asked for the bread, because I'm a great believer that you have not, because you ask not. And if you ask, you shall receive. I believe that."

Lucious found the poorest neighborhood in Indianapolis, pulled into the parking lot, and opened up the back of his van full of bread. That day was the beginning of his new ministry. A couple of years after Lucious had begun begging for food for the poor, he met two Catholic men who began to help him in his ministry, and they impressed him with their willingness to help.

Lucious was surprised. "I thought, Boy, what is God doing? Now I know two Catholics. I'd never met a Catholic before in my life."

Next, Lucious was introduced to Fr. Steve Schwab by his new Catholic friends. Fr. Steve invited Lucious to come to his parish.

"Father used to always say to me, 'Lucious, I really would love to give you Communion, but you understand I can't, don't you?' I said, 'Sure I do.' And he said, 'But I'm going to give you the gospel.'"

Fr. Steve and Lucious became good friends. Lucious studied and learned about the Catholic faith and eventually converted.

"The mother church is the Catholic Church. Everybody wants to be with the mother. And I consider the Catholic Church the mother of all churches," Lucious says.

Lucious has been in Indianapolis now for almost twenty years, working seven days a week at doing the Lord's work.

"I start begging by 4:15, 4:30. I go to produce houses. I get the very best. In an average day for me, I'll give away at least six thousand pounds of food."

Lucious doesn't feed just the poor; he also gives them money for rent or utilities, whatever they might be in need of. He gets the money for this charity by asking for it.

"I go at it," he says. "I tell everybody I'm serving Jesus."

Bill Bahler is one of the many volunteers who have been changed by coming to know Lucious. He heard him speak at his church about eight years ago.

Bill recalls their first meeting: "In comes Lucious, who happens to be a minority, wearing bib overalls in this real nice church we're in, front teeth missing, and he got up there and talked to us about his work and invited us down to see what he does. And he just mesmerized us. We were touched by his sincerity and by his commitment." Bill has been working with Lucious every Saturday since he first heard him speak.

"I really feel like I'm in the presence of an apostle," Bill says. "Everything he says and does, he's trying to let Christ speak for him. He's taught me discernment. As he would say, there's the needy and the greedy both in poor people as well as rich people. And we'll serve both down there, but we're not going to let the greedy take advantage of the needy."

Just feeding the poor wasn't enough for Lucious. He had a vision of starting a center in the poorest area of the city where people would have access to dental care, medical help, and educational services. Through amazing circumstances, he was given some land and decided to build.

"I broke the ground and my friends started laughing at me, saying, 'How you gonna do this?'" Lucious recalls. "And I said, 'My faith will build it.'"

And his faith did build the center through the generous donations of many people. The center is called Anna's House, named after Anna Molloy, one of Lucious' most fervent volunteers, despite her being ten years old, on oxygen support, and confined to a wheelchair. Lucious will tell you that the things he's done in his life have all pretty much been accomplished by adhering to one very simple way of thinking.

"Everything belongs to God," he says. "You just gotta ask Him for it, that's all. You just gotta ask Him. And He will give to you. He will."

Lucious Newsom passed away on August 19, 2008. Bill Bahler says that after meeting Lucious at a Bible study he felt called to join him at his Lord's Pantry Ministry and was blessed to serve with him for fifteen years until his death. Bill says about Lucious, "I saw the Lord lead him, saw miracles performed through his faith, and saw hundreds fed and served by this 'good and faithful servant.'" | Aired: October 9, 2006

***

Dying of Thirst

An African boy had a three-foot-long guinea worm removed from his leg—the result of a lack of clean water. As Brenda Koinis, from Houston, watched the scene unfold on screen, she was not only moved by what she saw. She was motivated to do something about it.

"It made me cry," says Brenda. "It alerted me to a whole body of suffering that I hadn't really paid attention to before. God used that image to pierce my heart. And it would have been a sort of 'feed a man a fish' kind of response for me to just make a donation. By my starting the H2O Project, it's more of an ongoing 'plant seeds and they keep on growing' kind of thing. And I think God gave me that idea and showed me that need right at a time in my life when I had time to act on it."

In 2001, Brenda founded the H2O Project, an amazingly simple idea to help people around the world share in the gift of clean water.

"It's a challenge to make a difference," she says. "The challenge is to make water your only beverage for two weeks. To eat normally, but to give up all those other beverages we can really do without, and then to take that money and use it to help provide clean water somewhere where people are dying because they don't have clean water to drink."

Brenda began by going to schools and churches and showing the video of the guinea worm to help open the eyes of those around her to the plight these people were facing. She would tell them that every fifteen seconds another child dies from a water-related illness and that each year water-related diseases kill more people than AIDS and cancer combined.

"Until you see a picture of what life with dirty water looks like, you really can't imagine it," Brenda says. "For most of these people it's not a matter of having *no* water, it's a matter of having water that is contaminated. None of us has had to go down to a stream—a stream where cows are defecating upstream and someone else is dumping their sewage and people are washing their clothes—and said, 'I will take this home, and this is what my family will drink today.' We just haven't come to an experience anywhere close to that."

Brenda has a website that offers educational and motivational supplies, without charge, to those who wish to take the H2O Challenge. She asks that the money saved then be sent directly to an organization already involved in bringing clean water to areas that need it.

"What we ask people to do is to select someone they trust to make use of the funds that they've raised. They can do that on their own. We also have on our website several organizations that we've checked out, that we have a relationship with, and that we feel confident will make good use of the funds. Living Water is based on the south side of Houston. Life Water is based in California. World Vision is in Washington. Catholic Relief Services provides water in more than one place, but right now they provide water to Ethiopia with the funds that are raised by the H2O Project."

Brenda has been surprised over the years that the H2O Project has been helping more than just those people who are in need of clean water.

"I thought that I was being called to do this just for the sake of the people in the world who need clean water," she says. "But it's really made a difference in the lives of people in the world who need to *give* clean water. There are two pretty interesting residual effects. One is a physical one. I've had several people come up to me and just tell me how different they felt physically after getting off all those other beverages for two weeks. Some of them sleep better or aren't as jittery or find that they're saving a lot of money. And then from a spiritual or a global-awareness aspect, the most common response that we get on our feedback form is that this has opened their eyes to the need somewhere else and to how much we have and how much we can do with what we have."

The number of people taking the H2O Challenge has continued to grow since Brenda first started the project.

"In Africa, on average, a dollar will give somebody clean water for a year. So you start doing that math and a lot of lives are being changed."

If you're looking for an easy way to help bring clean water to the world, get free materials to help you promote it, and not put out any more money than you already were putting out before you began the project, then Brenda's challenge is it.

"This project works for people of almost all ages and circumstances," Brenda says. "I've had retirees do it and I've had kindergarteners do it. The smallest gift can make a huge difference. And so none of us should be saying, 'Oh, well, I can't do much, so I won't do anything.' We should all be saying, 'I can't do much, but God can use what I can do.'"

Brenda Koinis is the founder and director of the H2O Project (www.theH20project.org). It is her hope that someday all will have clean water and that many will be healthy simply because those who live in abundance were willing to give up their beverages for two weeks every year. | Aired: March 2, 2009

✱ ✱ ✱
Moved to Action: Questions for Thought

1. Heidi Kühn's background as an international journalist exposed her to other countries and their plights. She took her experience to help those in other countries and put it into action. Where in the world are you drawn to put your efforts into helping others? Who is the neighbor you feel called to embrace?
2. Debbie Cornall feels that it's our duty to help children in Iraq. They deserve to have their needs met just as our own children do. Does your parish do any outreach in your own community? Is there someone in your parish who has a loved one in the military who needs assistance?
3. Lucious Newsom never met a stranger, and he ministered to anyone in need. How do you feel about his statement that "everything belongs to God; you just gotta ask Him for it, that's all. You just gotta ask Him. And He will give it to you. He will." Do you believe Lucious? For what have you asked God?
4. Brenda Koinis was moved by a video she saw of a suffering African boy. She took action to make a difference for his life and the lives of others living in that dire condition. What have you seen that moves you to take action? What is holding you back from getting started?

CHAPTER | SEVEN |

WOMB TO TOMB
Pro-life for All Life

For it was you who formed my inward parts;
you knit me together in my mother's womb.

—Psalm 139:13

Gabriel's Gift

Fifteen months after JoAnne Cascia delivered a healthy baby boy in 2003, she found out she was pregnant again, but she wasn't prepared for what the doctors had to say when she went in for a routine checkup.

"We didn't know there was anything wrong with Gabriel until our twenty-week ultrasound," JoAnne says. "He had something called thanatophoric skeletal dysplasia, which basically means that the bones are not growing at the rate that they should. The problem with the ribs not growing was that the chest cavity would not expand, and without expansion of the chest cavity there was no room for his lungs to develop. They told us we had to make a decision because this condition he had was not compatible with life."

JoAnne and her husband sought the advice of various medical specialists. They felt there had to be an alternative to ending the pregnancy right away. But the doctors didn't agree.

"Pretty much the overwhelming opinion of the medical community was that we should terminate," says JoAnne. "The doctor who was going to deliver him told me he would not deliver in the hospital where I was planning to have the baby. He said I was not allowed to have the baby there. So at five months, I started looking for a new doctor and a new hospital, because I felt strongly that I was not going to terminate the pregnancy."

Some doctors told JoAnne that her pregnancy would be considered high-risk to her, though not life-threatening. However, that wasn't the main reason they gave her.

"What they told me was, 'Why put yourself through four and a half more months of pregnancy when you don't have to?' That's essentially what they said, and my answer was, 'Well, because that's my baby.'

"My husband and I talked a lot about it, and we felt very, very strongly that we had signed on to be parents to this baby. If our only job as his parents was to see him through his life, however short it was, and make sure he went with peace and with dignity and surrounded by people who loved him, then we would have done our job as his parents. The only people who were telling us to terminate were the doctors. But everyone else in our lives—our friends, our family, coworkers, and others—everyone agreed with us that we should not terminate. I can only imagine how a younger girl, or someone who didn't have the support system I have, would have felt. She might have just done what the doctors recommended."

After searching for more than a month, JoAnne finally found St. Peter's, a Catholic hospital in New Brunswick, New Jersey, that supported her and her husband in their decision to continue the pregnancy.

"It was about our finding the right doctor and knowing that we were in the right place," JoAnne says. "I carried Gabriel to term. He was born February 24, 2004, and he lived for an hour and a half."

JoAnne invited her family and close friends to the hospital to be with her and her husband after the birth of Gabriel, who was delivered by C-section. The hospital even had food and drinks in the recovery room so that no one would have to leave after the birth. Gabriel was baptized, and JoAnne says he was kissed and loved for the entire hour and a half of his life.

"I felt that for some reason God had chosen us to be Gabriel's parents, and that maybe it was because He knew we would let him live his life and do what he needed to do," JoAnne explains. "So I kind of turned it around and looked at it as an honor instead of a punishment; I tried to look at it as God's way of choosing me and telling me I was such a good mom that He wanted to give me this very special job to do. And Gabriel did a really, really special thing. His birth and his short life have really touched a lot of people. There were more than two hundred people at his funeral."

JoAnne had wished she had someone to talk to when she was going through the difficult time with Gabriel, and eventually she found Pamela Houghton, who also experienced a pregnancy with a fatal prognosis.

"That's when we decided we had to start some type of a network so that other moms who are in the same situation can find people to talk to," says JoAnne. So she and Pamela started a ministry at the parish level—the Pieta Ministry—and eventually it moved to the diocesan level.

"The image of the Pietà, of Mary holding her dying son, was an image that we could relate to," says JoAnne. "And we thought that really kind of summed up exactly what all of these moms are feeling and going through."

JoAnne and Pamela give women who are going through tough times someone to talk to and someone who understands them in a very personal way. Women or mothers of girls having to face this kind of decision find a sympathetic and understanding ear. JoAnne also continues to speak to churches and other groups who want to hear her story.

"You always feel good when you're helping someone else, so if I can get up and talk to a group of people and one person in that group can relate to what I'm going through or can feel better about what they're going through because of what I have to say, then I feel it's worth it. And the other thing is that I think that as a mom you just always want to talk about your kids."

The courage shown by JoAnne and others who are faced with a fatal diagnosis for their baby is an inspiration for all of us to continue to see the good that God can do in seemingly hopeless situations. For support when there's a difficult diagnosis, go to www.benotafraid.net.

Gabriel Cascia's big brother, Patrick, is now in fourth grade. In 2010, JoAnne's husband, Dave, suffered a heart attack. He survived, but that same year they lost their home and everything they owned, including their pets, in a house fire. Throughout the trials they have continued to count their blessings rather than their losses. Their faith in God has remained constant, and their home was rebuilt. Although they lost almost everything in the fire, amazingly Gabriel's baptismal outfit, his candle, and their photo album of him were saved. | Aired: July 31, 2006

* * *

Choose Life, No Matter What

When nineteen-year-old Edel Carrick was invited to a party by a friend, she thought she was in for an evening of fun. It didn't turn out that way. At the party, unbeknownst to her, Edel was drugged and fell unconscious. In the morning, she awoke knowing that she had been sexually assaulted.

"I couldn't believe it," Edel says. "I knew what had happened. I was hurting badly, and even walking home was very painful."

Edel made it home, but she felt ashamed that she could have let this happen, so she didn't tell anyone about the incident until a month later, when she discovered she was pregnant.

"I was terrified," Edel recalls. "I didn't know what to do. My dad was the first person I went to. I talked to him and told him what had happened, and he asked me why I hadn't come to him sooner. I told him I was scared. I didn't know what to say. I didn't want to disappoint my parents."

Since Edel had not gone to the police right away, they told her the chances of apprehending the man who had done this were nearly nil, and they stopped the investigation a couple of months later. Edel was determined to move on. At this point you might expect a young girl who found herself pregnant after a brutal attack to consider abortion. But that was never an option for Edel.

"For a long time I didn't know what I was going to do," she says. "I knew I was not going to have an abortion, because that's just something I am very strong in my beliefs about. But I didn't know if I was going to keep the baby. I was talking to a few different places and people who helped with adoptions."

At her first visit to the doctor, Edel was told that she was permanently scarred from the attack and that, because she had juvenile diabetes, the pregnancy would be very risky.

"When the doctors told me there was a chance I wouldn't be able to have kids, I had that in the back of my mind. And this baby needed to have everything. He needed to have everything I couldn't give him. But when I felt him move for the first time, it was as if he were a part of me, a part that I could never give away."

Edel continued with her pregnancy, with the support of her parents and family, who knew she was going to keep the baby.

"The church and my family were really the only people who held me together, because I didn't know what I was going to do," Edel says. "And there wasn't a time after that happened that I wasn't praying that I would make the right decision; that I would know what I was supposed to do; that God would give me the strength and everything else I needed to carry this child through full term.

"I had a lot of complications, and even up until the end of my pregnancy it was kind of touch and go. There was a possibility that one or both of us wouldn't make it. At times, the doctors told me I shouldn't even go through with the pregnancy, and they advised that I have an abortion. Every time that came up, I told them, 'It's not the child's fault that this happened. And I'm not going to do that. I'm not going to take away, on a chance that I won't make it, the chance for this child to have a great life.'"

At seven and a half months into the pregnancy, Edel developed congestive heart failure. She had an extremely hard decision to make.

"The doctors told me, 'We need to take him out or you're not going to make it.' I think that was the scariest point for my parents, and they were there through everything. The doctors told me, 'If you're going to make it through this, we need to take the baby now.' I told them that if he wasn't ready to come out, they should leave him in longer. I told them that I'd had twenty years of a great life—parents who were always there for me, a family who supported me through everything—and I felt that this child deserved a chance. They said, 'Well, there's a chance he won't make it even if we leave him.' And I said I wanted him left in. I had to sign all kinds of papers that said no matter what, you're not taking him until he's ready."

Six doctors were there to attend the dangerous delivery. Edel eventually gave birth to Zachary, a 7-pound 15-ounce baby. He needed intensive care for a month until his lungs developed, but he is now a healthy, active little boy.

"I'm blessed and I'm lucky that he looks just like me," says Edel. "People told me, you're twenty years old and your life is over. But I told them my life is just beginning on a whole new level."

"I'm happier now than I've ever been in my whole life," says Edel.

Edel Carrick, in Phoenix, Arizona, is a pro-life speaker and works full-time at the Franciscan Renewal Center. She is a very happy mom and woman strong in her faith and pro-life beliefs. She has experienced extreme situations that have ended in the best part of her life and is grateful that God has given her the opportunity to help people understand the importance of life in any circumstance. Edel can be reached at www.edelschoice.com for speaking events and retreats. | Aired: September 3, 2007

***

ALWAYS LISTEN TO YOUR MOTHER

In 1991, Dr. John Bruchalski was doing his residency in obstetrics and gynecology at the Jones Institute for Reproductive Medicine in Norfolk, Virginia. During that time, he did things that he would never consider doing today.

"I did terminations during my residency," John says. "My professor told me that providing abortions was a lucrative part of medical practice. I wanted to provide good reproductive services for my patients, and I thought my providing abortions would help liberate them from their reproductive problems. But it quickly became clear just what I was doing. When you see the damage you do to the baby, you know what you're doing. And the problem for those women continued. They were still being used before and after the abortion—in other words, their relationships were the problems, and we were providing just one consequence of those bad relationships. I saw more and more of those women's hearts become hardened."

While on a mission trip to Guadalupe, Mexico, John visited the shrine of Our Lady of Guadalupe. There, he says, he heard something that changed his life and would cause him to tell his professors he could not continue performing abortions.

"I thought I heard a feminine voice say, 'Why are you hurting me?'" John recalls. "And it became very clear to me that I could not continue to provide abortions, and, in fact, that I actually had to do something to fight against it."

After having drifted away, John came back to the Catholic Church, in part because Church teachings regarding respect for life confirmed what he had been wrestling with inside. He then made another trip, this time to Medjugorje, in Bosnia and Herzegovina.

"When I went to Medjugorje, I heard something very clearly: 'In order for you to be successful, Johnny, you must practice excellent medicine, follow the teachings of my Son's Church, and serve the underserved in your daily experience. And with those three methods you will be able to transform hearts through health care.'"

John took those words to heart. In 1994 he started the Tepeyac Family Center and opened his doors to provide affordable health care to women—in particular, those with crisis pregnancies. In 2000 he began Divine Mercy Care as a nonprofit umbrella organization to help continue to fund and expand the center.

"The Arlington diocese is one of only three dioceses in the country that do not have Catholic health care," John explains. "So first we had an OB-GYN practice, and we knew there were other doctors who might be interested in joining us. There was also a gentleman who wanted to live his faith in his own work, in the pharmacy area. So we added the pharmaceutical piece to the health-care entity, Divine Mercy Care. We called it DMC Pharmacy, and it opened in October 2008. It's a place where professionals and patients can live their faith in the marketplace."

DMC Pharmacy carries no contraceptive products, such as birth control and morning-after pills and condoms, and they sell no pornography. The pharmacy maintains a pro-life environment and encourages natural family planning (NFP).

"We've had forty years now of living under the contraceptive lie of easy sex, of sex as a recreational sport," says John. "And we have also had forty years of improved NFP education and training. We now have crisis-pregnancy centers that are out in the community and trying to help. All the pieces of the puzzle are there. People are beginning to realize that they have to live integrated lives: body, soul, and spirit. They cannot be Catholic on Sundays and not try to live their faith during the week."

When DMC Pharmacy opened, Bishop Paul Loverde of Arlington was there to bless the new business. He said the pharmacy would provide a great service to the Catholic community as well as work to convert people to the pro-life cause, and that's just what John has been praying for.

"This is an opportunity for us to truly put meat and flesh to the bones of our faith," John says. "And in a world where there is so much confusion and so much dissent on conscience issues, I believe that the *Theology of the Body* and the teachings of the Catholic Church hold the secret to the renewal of the respect for human life. We are all called to holiness. This was not something special for me. If my example can help others live and become holy, so be it."

John Bruchalski's affiliations with the Couple to Couple League and the Family of the Americas Foundation make him one of the country's foremost medical experts on natural family planning. He has spoken on various topics concerning the renaissance of Catholic medicine here in the United States, in Canada, and in Europe. Dr. Bruchalski has been married to Carolyn since 1991 and is the father of two boys. | *Aired: January 19, 2009*

***

This Can't Be Happening

Forty-nine-year-old attorney Lisa Gigliotti from Lansing, Michigan, is uniquely qualified to speak out against assisted suicide and other anti-life practices. She's been living with chronic pain for more than two decades.

"At twenty years old I was a premed student," says Lisa. "I was robust and had a lot of determination to become a medical missionary. Then one night, I woke up in the middle of the night in a pain-locked ball. It was the kind of pain that makes you break out in a sweat and scream out loud. I was diagnosed with a fairly severe case of rheumatoid arthritis."

After receiving her diagnosis, Lisa drove directly to the house of her Italian grandmother, whom she called Nona. She knew Nona would know what to say to comfort her.

"Nona just said very quietly to me, '*Coraggio,* Leeza, *coraggio.*' She meant that I needed to have courage to deal with this."

Lisa was going to need to put that advice into action. In just a few short years she was bedridden. She moved in with her mother and grandmother, who took care of her. Then, as if dealing with her chronic pain wasn't challenge enough, Lisa's mother was killed in a car accident and her grandmother was seriously injured and, soon after, died as well.

"Believe it or not, just weeks after that, I began to get a lot of neuromuscular symptoms. I had double vision, my speech was slurred, my arms felt as if they each weighed a hundred pounds, and I was diagnosed with a second autoimmune disease called myasthenia gravis."

Lisa needed to receive a series of dialysis treatments, so she was placed in a nursing home to receive the help she needed and to be close to the hospital. As soon as the dialysis was complete, she couldn't wait to get out of the nursing home.

"I believe it was purely by the grace of God that right out of the nursing home I was able to receive two new artificial knees and I could walk again," Lisa says.

Lisa wasted no time; almost as soon as she was up walking again, she began taking a course to become a hospital chaplain. And then, knowing that her dream of becoming a medical missionary was not possible, she instead went to law school.

"Right out of law school I started as an attorney representing people with disabilities," says Lisa. "Around the same time, in our state, Jack Kevorkian became active. It was an interesting argument that Kevorkian and the right-to-die advocates were making. It was that the best solution and the kindest, most humane solution is to help seriously ill, suffering people to die, because then they will no longer have any pain. So an interesting revelation from God is, 'You are now a woman who has survived two serious illnesses. They affect your everyday life. You have pain every day of your life. You will struggle to move your body with a neuromuscular disease the rest of your life, and yet you've never felt this need to end your life. What is the difference?'

"I then prayed a lot and decided I really had to do something about this, even though it perhaps wasn't going to be the popular thing to do."

At this time, Lisa was working in the Michigan senate and was able to be directly involved and to speak publicly about her views on life issues such as assisted suicide, cloning, and partial-birth abortion.

"I encountered an incredible amount of public scorn," says Lisa. "Jack Kevorkian was, in my estimation, taking people's lives, the majority of whom were women. And most of them did not have a terminal illness. Most people don't know that."

In the past, there were not as many doctors specializing in pain management as there are today. Finding the right doctor to take care of your particular situation was not always easy; Lisa knows that firsthand, after having been through ten surgeries herself. But she's convinced that ending a life is never the right answer.

"One of my messages for people with regard to assisted suicide is to never give up hope. There's always an option out there."

Lisa continues to work tirelessly to bring about a culture of life. She's written four books about her journey with pain and shares the wisdom that she's come to understand through it all. She emphasizes how crucial it is to have a strong faith life filled with *coraggio*, as her grandmother said.

"Our faith is so important," Lisa says. "You may struggle when you're diagnosed with some illness or experiencing the daily chronic pain or chronic frustration that results from your body not following through with what you need it to do. But God is always there and always present and always benevolent. It really is incumbent on every one of us every day to act with kindness toward others, especially toward those who are suffering."

Lisa Gigliotti has forged successful careers as an administrative-law judge and manager, a policy advisor for the Michigan state senate and governor, and an advocate for people with disabilities and for improving end-of-life care. She is dedicated to helping others lead more fulfilling lives. Lisa has written four books that describe her coraggio *and is the founder of With Courage I Can, whose mission is to encourage others through the Coraggio! books. Join in the conversation at http://withcourageican.com. | Aired: January 17, 2011*

***
"You Do It." "Who, Me?"

It's always amazing to see how just *one* person answering God's call can affect an entire community, and even the world, in big ways. Consider Mother Teresa, who spent her life helping the dying in India. She began her Missionaries of Charity ministry by simply picking up one dying man on a street in Calcutta. Now consider Karen Bussey, from Lansing, Michigan, who is doing something similar in her own community.

"My profession is social work," says Karen. "And I worked in hospice. Having worked in hospice, I was aware of the need that people had for someone to help take care of them at home. I also knew how financially stretched a family could become when a loved one was dying. And finances weren't the only concerns. Many times a small family would become exhausted and need physical and mental support. Unfortunately, that was pretty common."

Throughout her life, Karen has always admired the work of Mother Teresa. She feels she can relate in many ways to her vocation. "A very personal connection for me is that we're both consecrated," says Karen. "I am a consecrated virgin in the world. A lot of people may be unfamiliar with what that means. It's an ancient vocation that's recently been renewed. Mother Teresa was consecrated in religious life, and she would talk about her love for Jesus as her spouse. The heart of my own vocation, a spousal love for the Lord, mirrors that of Mother Teresa."

Karen knew there were things she wished were different in caring for the dying. She was intimately familiar with how the system worked, and she wanted it to change. She envisioned some kind of home for the dying there in Michigan, but she felt she couldn't do anything about it. She was just one person with a good idea and nowhere to go with it. At least that's what she thought.

"There was a time when I was particularly taking more time in prayer," she says. "This was not to pray about any specific ministry. This was not to solve problems or discern about this issue at all. I just wanted to spend more time with God. I wasn't prepared for what happened next. I felt like somewhere out of the blue God said to me, 'You do it.' And immediately I knew. I knew He was talking about the house for the terminally ill."

This was not in Karen's plans or comfort zone. Karen argued that "my work was clinical. I would help with counseling, but I was not a community organizer. I didn't have an administrative background. I didn't have a house to bring people to. I didn't have funds. I didn't have influential contacts. So it never occurred to me that I would do something about this. But Mother Teresa's example gave me courage. She gave me the courage to just start."

Karen gathered some of her Catholic friends together to help her start forming the ministry. She began with the simple idea that she wanted to help take care of the dying. In 1997, after nine months of planning, she became the founder and director of a home that provides care for people with terminal illnesses.

"During the end of those nine months, my friends and I began praying about what name to give the house. That same week we were praying, Mother Teresa died, on September 5, 1997. And so I knew I had the answer. The house would be called Mother Teresa House. This new house for the dying, named after Mother Teresa, was born at the same time that she died."

Although the Diocese of Lansing couldn't offer financial help, the bishop offered Karen the use of a house the diocese owned. This helped tremendously, since Mother Teresa House doesn't ask its guests to pay. They depend solely on donations from individuals, churches, service groups, and businesses to cover operating expenses. They also have a large corps of volunteers who step in to care for the guests.

Karen explains: "For terminally ill guests we are using three rooms on the first floor. We call them our guests. They come to live here. Their hospice agencies visit them here, but we are the ones who are with them twenty-four hours a day. We have a live-in volunteer program. So many, many people after me have taken a turn living here and serving full-time. But also there's a group of seventy people from the community here who take turns giving care.

"What the sick person needs are the little things. And that's what Mother Teresa teaches us. Do the little things. Care for one person at a time. It's the little things, like getting the person a drink of water or remembering when it's time for them to take their medicine, that make a difference in a life."

Mother Teresa House can care for up to three people at a time. Since they opened the house they have cared for close to two hundred people.

"Most of the time we have three people here. That seems to be so little compared to how many are in our community. But it makes a big impact. Because of all the many people who are trained here, hundreds then go home and help someone else. They can help somebody they know in their family or in their neighborhood and not be afraid to touch the sick.

"And now there are seven homes just in Michigan that use various aspects of our model at Mother Teresa House. So many are being cared for just by us doing our little thing that we think God asked us to do. What a joy it is to be in this community of people who just want to give something of themselves freely. It's truly a house full of love."

Karen Bussey is a consecrated virgin in the Catholic Church. She lives in Lansing, Michigan, and is founder and director of Mother Teresa House for the Care of the Terminally Ill. To learn more, go to www.motherteresa-house.org. | Aired: August 23, 2010

***

MOVED TO ACTION: QUESTIONS FOR THOUGHT

1. JoAnne Cascia and her husband made a difficult decision to keep their baby even though they knew he wouldn't live. What do you think about what they went through? How does what they did reinforce the pro-life message?

2. Amazing courage and determination were shown by Edel Carrick when she was faced with a horrible situation. She was determined to not let her child be punished for the crimes of others. How does her story bring light to the argument that abortion should be legal in the case of rape? What do you think about it? Could you do what Edel did?

3. Dr. John Bruchalski faced contemporary society head-on by not prescribing birth control. It is an unpopular stance to take and could have threatened his livelihood. What lesson can you learn from his willingness to follow God's will and not his own?

4. "Thou shalt not kill" is not meant to pertain just to babies in the womb. Lisa Gigliotti shows us that every human being, whether old, infirm, suffering, or young, has worth. Are you aware of the laws about euthanasia in your state? Do you feel called to find out and speak up about this issue?

5. Karen Bussey answered the call to help the dying in her community by starting the Mother Teresa House for the dying. Are there elderly in your own parish communities who have been forgotten? Have you ever felt that you couldn't do something because you were just one person? How does Karen's story affect you?

CHAPTER | EIGHT |

FOR THE LEAST OF THESE
Living Justly Today

And the king will answer them, "Truly I tell you, just as you did it to one of the least of these who are members of my family, you did it to me."

—Matthew 25:40

BUILDING A SIMPLE HOUSE

Thirty-one-year-old Clark Massey wasn't always dedicated to working and living with the poor. In fact, high finance was more what his family had in mind. Clark had been working on his Ph.D. in finance for a few years when he felt called to leave and go into missionary work.

"That was an interesting time," Clark recalls. "I tried to explain my desire to my family and my Ph.D. advisor, and I didn't even know how that desire was going to be realized."

Clark decided to complete his master's degree in finance and take a job in landscape construction in Tucson.

"I really felt called to get to know the poor," Clark says. "If there was an evangelization field for me, that's where I wanted to be. But I had a hard time convincing anybody else that that was a good vocation for me."

Although he enjoyed working with the poor in Tucson, with more than twenty thousand dollars in college loans, Clark needed to earn more than the minimum wage that the landscaping business paid. He got a job as an economist in Washington, D.C., and paid off his debt. Then, instead of banking the extra money he made there, he quit his job and moved into a homeless shelter to help as a volunteer and learn from them how to serve the poor.

"I wanted to do something in a very personal way," Clark explains. "I wanted to go into the areas where I didn't see people going to help, actually go into the projects and meet some of these single moms and see what the situation was there. That's where the idea of A Simple House started to form.

"The question was how to take this kind of 'personal' friendship approach we'd done at the soup kitchen and expand it to create authentic friendships with families who were struggling in the poorest areas of D.C. It's hard to know whether you're really following God or not in starting something like this, or if it's just a wild, harebrained idea."

Clark persisted with his idea and formed a nonprofit organization. He recruited people interested in his mission to form a board of directors and found volunteers ready to serve the poor in a new and innovative way. They raised funds and, on December 31, 2003, they got their first house, in southeast D.C. Clark and a few dedicated volunteers moved into it, in one of the city's poorest neighborhoods. Since most people living in the projects and in Section 8 housing aren't able to travel, Clark felt the best way to evangelize and befriend these people was to live with them.

"We have a food pantry in the house and we deliver the groceries," Clark says. "We don't have people pick them up. And we also use the house for full-time volunteers to live in, and we host a lot of different things in the house."

Clark now has two houses, five full-time volunteers, and plenty of part-time people eager to help with his ministry.

"We're entirely funded by individual donors, and we send out a newsletter only four times a year," he says. "That has been enough to fund our whole operation over the last four years. We're always trying to live by divine providence. If we have a lot of money, we do more ministries. If we don't have a lot of money, well, then, we do more Bible studies and less food delivery, so it all kind of balances out."

"We're trying to marry the corporal and the spiritual works of mercy. We're trying to give love to the poor in a way that we are delivering friendship, truth, faith, and hope. At the same time, if they are in dire need of something or maybe just need something like bus fare, we're also delivering that kind of material help. But we're doing it in the context of relationship and friendship. And we call it friendship evangelization."

Clark knows his ministry is making a difference, even if the rewards seem slow in coming.

"It is a very long road," he says. "These neighborhoods are really rough, and a lot of the families we see have many different hardships. Fatherhood is almost unheard of around here, and finding a married couple when we go to a door is also rare. We're trying especially to honor the dignity of moms who are struggling to raise these kids in the roughest neighborhoods, with the worst school system, and with the worst crime, without many resources."

What keeps Clark and his full-time volunteers going is their strong devotion to their faith lives.

"Every day we have Morning Prayer together," says Clark. "We require that everybody go to Mass every day. That is usually done together, but it doesn't need to be. And we have Evening Prayer on our own. We make sure everyone keeps up with their prayer lives. We are really just active parishioners. We're parishioners at a church down here, and we're trying to get people into the parish community. We're trying to create that seamless transition between us and the parish. And I feel that this type of work should be going on at some level in the life of any parish."

Clark Massey has a master's degree in finance and worked as an economist before starting A Simple House in 2003. He is the general director of A Simple House and works as a missionary at Kansas City House. Find more stories in archived newsletters at www.asimplehouse.org. | Aired: June 2, 2008

***
Home Away From Home

Twenty-four-year-old Tina Marquart from Washington, Missouri, was all set to teach elementary school when she graduated from college. Instead, she listened to her friend, an assistant campus minister, who suggested she try something a little different and experience some volunteer work first.

"She encouraged me to consider doing volunteer work," says Tina. "I thought it would be a good experience and that it would also look good on a résumé, so I decided to check it out. But as it turned out, the experience took me down a completely different road."

Tina began her volunteer work at Nazareth Farm in West Virginia, and she quickly became hooked on the feeling of working in a community for and with other people.

"Nazareth Farm is a nonprofit home-repair organization that offers interest-free loans to low-income families who are in need of home repair," Tina says. "We would do the work and help the staff. Volunteers came from all over the country."

After a little over a year at Nazareth Farm, Tina accepted a job nearby in the little town of Alderson, West Virginia, where she could continue her love for nonprofit work. Alderson, a town of about a thousand, is located near Federal Prison Camp Alderson, which coincidentally holds around a thousand inmates. Tina's new job was to be the director of the Alderson Hospitality House.

"The house was started in 1977 by a couple who moved from the D.C. area," Tina explains. "They wanted to set up a place where lodging, meals, transportation, and general assistance and support could be offered to the family and friends of those serving time in the women's prison camp. The spirit behind it was that of the Catholic Worker

Movement. We don't require anybody to pay us anything. We run strictly on donations. Knowing that they don't have to pay $75 a night plus meals plus transportation back and forth to the prison brings these family members peace of mind, and I'm humbled to be able to offer that to folks. We have guests come from a thousand miles away and guests who are from in-state; we work to build community and see that they are not on this journey by themselves."

With the help of three full-time volunteers, Tina keeps the three-story, ten-bedroom house cleaned and maintained for up to fifty-five people. She also cooks meals for the families and tends to the grounds.

"It offers such a gift to the families to be able to see their loved ones, and for the inmates to know they are being supported through this challenging and difficult time. It's so important for the inmates, too, because we are called to be mindful of the prisoners as if we are sharing their prison with them. Typically around 10 percent of the prisoners get visitors; that's such a small number to begin with, and I believe that if the house wasn't here that number would go below 1 percent."

Moving to a small town without much nightlife or big-city offerings wasn't that difficult for Tina, but moving away from her family was. The decision to move to a locale that didn't allow her to simply run home on the weekends and see her siblings and parents was a difficult one, but she's confident she made the right choice.

"In some ways I feel very much in solidarity with the women at the camp who don't get to see their families every day like they used to," she says.

Not everyone could do what Tina does: meeting new people all the time, catering to their physical and emotional needs, and finding time for herself. But she feels blessed to have the job that she does, living in solidarity with families in need.

"I'm so happy to have the chance to wake up every day and know that I'm going to do something I absolutely love, which is cleaning and baking and being with people, encouraging people and supporting people. I love meeting new people. It never intimidates me to have a guest who's never been here before, because each of us has our own story. I think all we really want to do is just share it with someone. Knowing that I'm going to be here around folks doing something that's genuinely a ministry and a blessing to people is pretty life-giving. It makes it real easy to get up in the morning. And I praise God and thank Him for blessing me with this opportunity."

A Missouri native, Tina Marquart has spent the last five years loving and exploring the beauty of West Virginia. Her hope is to continue to love and serve and be inspired by the good and God around and within us. | Aired: October 13, 2008

***

Takin' It to the Streets

The word *homeless* can sometimes conjure up the image of an older, bearded, dirty-looking man sleeping on a park bench. Most of us wouldn't think of young men walking the streets and surviving as prostitutes. But this is exactly the population that Deacon John Green targeted when he founded Emmaus Ministries in Chicago.

Deacon John explains the problem: "When you start talking about male prostitution, it really confronts a lot of different things: our sense of masculinity, our sense that, well, men won't do that because they can just go get a job. As I began to hear these guys' stories and get into their lives, I recognized that the solution wasn't as simple as just getting a job to get out of it. Most men involved in prostitution don't even know who their fathers are, let alone have an intact family. Most of them dropped out of school by the fourth or fifth grade. Most of them experienced some form of sexual abuse or early sexual experience, generally between the ages of seven and eleven. And when you start adding all those factors together, the safety net is gone. They just don't have that. So what catches them is the streets. And the streets are a very vicious parent."

The purpose of Emmaus Ministries is to reach men involved in sexual exploitation and provide hope for them by developing ministries of evangelization, transformation, and education that's Christ-centered.

"These guys need proximity," says Deacon John. "I call it the three *T*s; time, touch, and talk. If you can give that to somebody who's on the streets, somebody who's homeless, somebody who's involved in prostitution, then you begin to have that sense of proximity. And it's in proximity that you can begin to help a person walk a different path."

Emmaus is funded by individual churches, both Catholic and Protestant foundations, and many individual donors and fund-raisers. They receive little government assistance. There are fifteen full-time and part-time employees on staff, along with some fifty volunteers.

"We have male/female teams that go out, sometimes multiple teams," Deacon John says. "We go into bars and clubs, on streets, in parks, different places where men are involved with prostitution, and we really just try to be present to guys."

John has noticed that the age of the men prostituting themselves, which used to be around twenty-five to thirty-five years, has continued to get younger during the eighteen years he's worked in this ministry.

"In the last six or seven years, we've seen a lot more thirteen-, fourteen-, and fifteen-year-old kids prostituting [themselves]."

"There was one young kid, Jamal, who was hustling. He was about fifteen years old. One day one of our staffers, Larry, who had actually come off the streets himself, confronted him. 'Are you tired of just being these guys' plaything out here?' Larry asked him. Jamal looked at Larry and then walked away. Larry was worried that he'd blown it by being too confrontational. A week later, Jamal and another man drove up to where Larry and a college volunteer were doing outreach. Jamal approached Larry, accompanied by the large man who'd come with him. Jamal pointed at Larry, and Larry heard him say, 'He's the one. He's the one.' The two walked up to Larry, and the unknown man stuck his hand out and began shaking Larry's hand. 'Thank you,' the man said. 'I want to thank you for sending my son home.'"

Emmaus offers these boys and men a place to feel safe and gives them the tools and support they need to make a change in their lives.

"As we meet guys through outreach, we encourage them to come into our drop-in center," Deacon John says. "It's a home—a kind of surrogate home. Every Wednesday we do a big family dinner, and a number of years ago a man named Joseph came in for one of our meals. In the midst of all the preparation, Joseph leaned over to me and quietly said, 'You know, John, I've never done this before.' 'What are you talking about?' I asked him. He looked around and said, 'This family-dinner thing; I've seen it on TV, but I've never done it before.' Here was a twenty-nine-year-old guy who never in his life had had a family dinner. That's what I see with these guys. They may have never had that true sense of family, but there's something innate within us that yearns for a place to call home. And that's what we try to create for them."

Emmaus Ministries is a shining example of how one man's mission to reach out to those looked over by many has inspired other helping hands to create a home for those who never had one before.

Deacon John Green has worked with homeless young people in Guatemala and Mexico and on the streets of New York and in Chicago, where he came to understand the acute need for long-term support for men in prostitution. Family commitments recently called Green to Ohio, where he is currently director of Catholic Charities Community Services in Summit County. But the work of Emmaus continues in Chicago as well as at its sister organization in Houston. Learn more at www.streets.org. | Aired: March 16, 2009

***
Who's Watching the Kids?

A terribly disturbing news story came out of Cincinnati in the summer of 2006. The disappearance of three-year-old foster child Marcus Fiesel brought out thousands of people to help in the search for him at the park where his foster mother had said he'd been lost. This search lasted almost eleven days. Holly Schlaack, who has worked with foster kids for almost fifteen years, was following the story closely.

"What we learned later was that the foster parents had actually murdered him," Holly says.

"They were going out of town to a family reunion and did not want to take Marcus with them. Instead, they bound him with packing tape and a blanket, wrapped him up like a mummy, and left him in a closet in 90-degree heat. He essentially died of hyperthermia. When they came home and found him dead, the foster father and his girlfriend burned his body. When it failed to burn entirely they dumped the remains in the Ohio River. And he was a foster child. He was a child placed in foster care for his protection. He had already been abused and neglected."

"To me, we can't let his story end there. We have to find a way to make it better for the half a million foster children across America who are in foster care right now. They are in every community across our nation, and we have to come together and find ways to help them."

Holly, who has three children of her own, has been representing the best interests of abused and neglected children in juvenile court, serving as a guardian ad litem (GAL) at ProKids in Cincinnati.

"ProKids is a court-appointed special-advocate program and part of a larger national movement," Holly says. "What we do at ProKids is recruit, train, and supervise community volunteers to advocate on behalf of abused and neglected children in juvenile court. Our goal at ProKids is to bring the community into the lives of children who desperately need a voice or an advocate. So our volunteers get to know as much as they can about these kids, and then they go into court and advocate for them during juvenile-court proceedings."

After the tragedy of Marcus Fiesel, Holly felt she had to do something to educate others about the crises facing foster children and to empower people to become a part of the solution. She wrote a book called *Invisible Kids: Marcus Fiesel's Legacy*.

"My hope really was to take Marcus's experience and find a way to bring good from it," Holly says. "I wanted to find a way to engage the community in helping the rest of the kids who are still here. The foster-care system sometimes works and sometimes fails."

Holly's Catholic upbringing helps her to handle the stress that comes along with this type of work. "I was raised in a home where our Catholic faith was an integral part of our family's lifestyle," she says. "And my mother, who is an amazing woman, she just really role-modeled for me and my five siblings the importance of service to other people. We are not here in this world to take care just of ourselves. We're here to take care of each other. We're here to take care of the people who need us."

Through research and day-to-day experience, Holly knew that the youngest of the foster kids were the most vulnerable. In 2000 she developed a program at ProKids called Building Blocks, which promotes advocacy for abused and neglected infants and toddlers.

"Children under the age of five are coming into foster care at rates faster than older children nationally," she says. "That's a critical time of rapid brain development and cognitive, social, and emotional growth. It really sets the stage and impacts so strongly the course of a child's life. So I thought if we could intervene and give impeccable advocacy to that young age group at that critical time, could we maybe in ten years start to see a different generation of kids?"

Holly wants everyone to know that these foster kids are out there, but they aren't visible to most of us.

"I think that when we start to understand that those kids are here and we learn about the issues they face, then from there we figure out what we can do and what's on our heart to do. The last chapter of my book outlines a dozen ways that the average person can make a difference. And you don't have to foster or adopt to do that. I would love to write a second book. And I would love my second book to be about how we as a community got behind our kids—telling how we pulled together even in these difficult economic times."

By living out her faith, Holly is answering the call to help these children who don't have a voice.

"As a mother, as a woman, I have a job in this world to do whatever I can for children who can't speak for themselves, who can't help themselves. And I really believe that I must do the piece that I can do and I have to be OK with that. I have to trust that He'll lead me where I'm supposed to go and ultimately, hopefully, that will bring good to our world."

Holly Schlaack is the author of Invisible Kids: Marcus Feisel's Legacy. *She has represented the best interests of abused and neglected infants and toddlers as a guardian ad litem in juvenile court and has extensive experience supervising court-appointed special advocates. She trains nationally on topics related to court advocacy as well as the power of community to impact lasting change for children and families. Holly and her husband live in Cincinnati with their three children. You can learn more at www.invisiblekidsthebook.com.* | *Aired: March 23, 2009*

***

A LITTLE TENDER LOVING CARE

Fifty-two-year-old Alice Wold from Phoenix is a mother of six and a former dentist. Her mother died when Alice was just ten years old, and at the age of thirty-six Alice suffered a stroke that left her unable to continue her dental practice. Instead of becoming bitter about what life had handed her, she viewed her challenges as blessings.

"Each one of those things has brought great blessings and empathy and compassion for other people—and appreciation for everything that I have," says Alice. "You realize that things you didn't think were important to people are. And even in your littleness you can be very helpful."

Alice finds many ways to be helpful in her parish. She and her husband teach RCIC, the Rite of Christian Initiation for Children. She also coordinates perpetual adoration, is active in the Serra Club, which fosters vocations in the Church, and is most active in the Christ Child Society.

"The Christ Child Society is a charitable organization of members dedicated to serving at-risk children regardless of race or creed," says Alice. "The Society was founded by Mary Virginia Merrick, who was injured when she was a teenager and was basically bedridden. She started the Christ Child Society in a small way by making a layette for a mom who was having a baby at Christmastime and didn't have clothes for her baby. Mary Virginia Merrick dedicated her whole life to giving to others despite the fact that she was an invalid."

In May of this year, Alice will become the president of her chapter of the Christ Child Society in Phoenix. "Mainly we help the poor," she says. "But we help out in schools also. To encourage love of reading, we have a book club for children. We have a layette program. We make comfort quilts for children's wards, little angel gowns for stillborn children, and bedtime bags for children going into foster homes. We help out with the Baby Shots program at the Phoenix fire department and Mission of Mercy, which is a free medical-van clinic that helps the underinsured. We just help wherever we can to meet the needs of children. And we try to do it with a little extra special tender loving care."

One of Alice's favorite activities of the Society is helping to make clothing for children and babies who are in need. "It's kind of like a sweatshop when we get together," says Alice. "We make it all, from receiving blankets to Onesies, undershirts, hooded bath towels, sweater sets, and afghans. So there are knitting, crocheting, and sewing machines going on. And we make it all from scratch. It's really cool. We meet here in Ahwatukee with about thirty women and at one more site up in Mount Claret, which is on Camelback Mountain, with about sixty women. Before I joined, I knew how to knit and crochet and do some sewing, but it's been wonderful for me because I've learned so much more, and they just teach me each step of the way."

Two times a month the groups get together to sew up a storm. All ages participate, from women in their thirties to some regulars who are in their nineties.

"We have our Christ Child prayer that we pray every time we get together," Alice says. "And when I'm making afghans, I interject a little prayer every once in a while for the Holy Spirit to guide the baby who will use it as they're growing. I hope it will bring them closer to God and help meet their needs. I think a lot of us have our own special private prayers that we pray while we're sewing or crocheting."

Alice continues: "We've talked with the nurses at the hospitals and it's just amazing. They say that some of these women come in with absolutely nothing.

"Sometimes there are tears in their eyes when they get this huge bag full of goodies. And it's all handmade, so that makes it extra special."

Alice and the Christ Child Society are making a big impact in people's lives by doing something that may seem insignificant. Alice reflects: "Giving back is just so important. And it's kind of interesting, because Christ presents so many paradoxes. You think you should seek for yourself and that you will find happiness in seeking for yourself, but in essence you really find happiness when you seek for others and you put yourself aside. Going outside yourself and being centered on others just enriches your life immensely."

Alice Wold continues to be an active member of the Christ Child Society by doing what she loves best: sewing, knitting, and making clothes for children and babies in need. She also loves to visit Catholic schools through the Book Club Buddies program of the Christ Child Society—reading to and helping children grow in their love of books. Alice and her husband continue to teach RCIC at Corpus Christi Catholic Church, where Alice coordinates perpetual adoration. | Aired: March 9, 2009

* * *
Moved to Action: Questions for Thought

1. Clark Massey takes his ministry to the people he serves and lives among. Have you ever felt called to serve the poor in your area? Does your parish reach out to others in your neighborhood?
2. Tina Marquart put her career on hold and instead gave her time for others in the prison system. How do you feel about ministering to the families of women in prison? Have you ever thought of these people when you read the Gospel expression "the least of these?"
3. Deacon John Green is reaching out to a population that isn't much talked about: male prostitutes. How does John's determination to get them help inspire you?
4. "We are not here in this world to take care just of ourselves." Holly Schlaack says her mother inspired her to care for others while she was growing up. How do you feel about that statement? Who do you take care of in your world? Are there more people you could include?
5. Alice Wold likes to do little things that make a big difference. What little thing have you done recently that has made a difference in someone else's life? If you haven't done anything, what can you do?

CONCLUSION

ONE MORE THOUGHT BEFORE YOU GO

Now that you have read about ordinary people doing some extraordinary things to make an impact on this world, think about what you might be able to do. We aren't all called to go to Haiti and work with the poor or start a homeless shelter in our home. But I'm sure there's something that you can do. As Patricia Oetting likes to recall, Mother Teresa said, "Don't wait for a leader. Do it yourself, person to person." The men and women in these stories weren't superheroes or super saints. They were people like you and me, with commitments, jobs, families, and the pressures of everyday life bearing down on them. But they listened to God, answered the call, and followed His will for their lives. I encourage you to do the same.

If you know someone who is living out his or her Catholic faith in a way that inspires and moves you, let me know about it at jzarick@franciscanmedia.org. Maybe together we can share it with others on *American Catholic Radio* and watch them be moved by faith.

—Judy